CULTURE SHOCK!

Belgium

Mark Elliott

Graphic Arts Center Publishing Company
Portland, Oregon

In the same series

Argentina	*Egypt*	*Laos*	*Sri Lanka*
Australia	*Finland*	*Malaysia*	*Sweden*
Austria	*France*	*Mauritius*	*Switzerland*
Belgium	*Germany*	*Mexico*	*Syria*
Bolivia	*Greece*	*Morocco*	*Taiwan*
Borneo	*Hong Kong*	*Myanmar*	*Thailand*
Britain	*Hungary*	*Nepal*	*Turkey*
California	*India*	*Netherlands*	*UAE*
Canada	*Indonesia*	*Norway*	*Ukraine*
Chile	*Iran*	*Pakistan*	*USA*
China	*Ireland*	*Philippines*	*USA—The South*
Cuba	*Israel*	*Scotland*	*Venezuela*
Czech Republic	*Italy*	*Singapore*	*Vietnam*
Denmark	*Japan*	*South Africa*	
Ecuador	*Korea*	*Spain*	

Barcelona At Your Door
Chicago At Your Door
Havana At Your Door
Jakarta At Your Door
Kuala Lumpur, Malaysia At Your Door
London At Your Door
New York At Your Door

Paris At Your Door
Rome At Your Door
San Francisco At Your Door

A Globe-Trotter's Guide
A Parent's Guide

A Student's Guide
A Traveler's Medical Guide
A Wife's Guide
Living and Working Abroad
Working Holidays Abroad

Illustrations by TRIGG

Photo credits: Betty Elliott (213), Mark Elliott (13, 44, 55, 68,100, 109, 137, 142, 152, 162, 194, 201, 208, 210, 216, 226), Dani Systermans (133), and Jo Systermans (53, 117, 172, 175, 177, 199, 203).

© 2001 Times Media Private Limited

This book is published by special
arrangement with Times Media Private Limited
Times Centre, 1 New Industrial Road, Singapore 536196
International Standard Book Number 1-55868-606-1
Graphic Arts Center Publishing Company
P.O. Box 10306 • Portland, Oregon 97296-0306 • (503) 226-2402

Printed in Singapore

National Library Board (Singapore)
Cataloguing in Publication Data

Elliott, Mark.
Culture Shock! : Belgium / Mark Elliott.
– Singapore : Times Books International, 2001. p. cm.
– (Culture Shock!)
Includes bibliographical references and index.
ISBN : 981-232-1934

1. Etiquette – Belgium. 2. Belgium – Description and travel.
3. Belgium – Social life and customs.
I. Title. II. Series: Culture Shock!

DH418   949.3 — dc21   SLS2001036924

CONTENTS

Chips, Chocolate, and Mussels   122

The Land of Beer   146

Business and Work   164

Entertainment and the Arts   170

Celebrations and Events   193

Where to Go? **205**

ACKNOWLEDGMENTS

This book is dedicated to the memory of Jo Systermans (Hermont), who sadly didn't live long enough to see it published.

Thirty thousand thank you's to Dani Systermans without whom I wouldn't have come to Belgium in the first place and certainly couldn't have written this book. Her inspiration, support, and kindness (in not making me eat those Brussels sprouts), are beyond measure. Unending thanks too to my unbeatable family across the Channel, to Wieland de Hoon for his patience and beer stamina, to Kris, Beverly, Marc, Dominique, Stella & Pierre, Deedee, Carine, Karine, the staff at Waterloo OTSI, and dozens of other people who have helped me experience and enjoy this country so much more. May your chips never want for mayonnaise.

NORTH
SEA

THE NETHERLANDS

Knokke
(Knokke-Heist)

Ostend • Damme
• Bruges

Veurne

Schoten • Turnhout

Sint-Niklaas ■ Antwerp

Lier • ANTWERP

■ Gent

FLANDERS

WEST
FLANDERS

EAST FLANDERS

Poperinge
• Ieper • Kortrijk

Oudenaarde

Mechelen • Aarschot

LIMBURG

• Hasselt

Louvain
Brussels •

Anderlecht • Uccle

BRABAN

Sint-Truiden

Overijse

Tongeren

Halle • Waterloo • Wavre

Braine-l'Alleud

Liège ■ • Herve

Tournai

Ath
•

HAINAUT

Nivelles

LIÈGE

Eupen

Mons
•

Binche

Namur •

Huy •

Spa •

Jemappes
•

■ Charleroi

N

Dinant •

Saint-Vith •

ARDENNES

NAMUR

Saint-Hubert •

FRANCE

• Bastogne

ARDENNES

LUXEMBOURG

LUXEMBOURG

• Bouillon

Arlon •

GERMANY

BELGIUM

9

INTRODUCTION

Unlike many of the more obviously exotic countries covered by books in this series, Belgium is a place that carefully shields visitors from the most immediate forms of culture shock. On the surface things seem very straightforward. The people are practical, multilingual, and obliging. As an English speaker, you'll be able to get by without learning the languages and without leaving the comfortable confines of a multinational expatriate environment. Then three years later, you discover that your apparently levelheaded neighbor sneaks out to carnivals dressed in a barrel costume, boggle-eyed mask, and tarantula hat to throw oranges at passers by. Or that his smart university student daughter spends unashamed hours reading comic books. That his wife drinks beer flavored with raspberries. That they all rave about holidays on one of Europe's most rainy, concrete blighted beaches. Belgium takes a perverse pleasure in its "boring" image—an image which it fosters, perhaps, to make it seem ideally suited as the capital of Europe. But underneath, the culture is a unique, complex, and intriguing blend: proud but not nationalistic, friendly but reserved, accommodating yet obstinate. And practical in its approach to almost any issue. This book helps you uncover the real Belgium, and to help you make the most of your time amongst Europe's most underestimated people.

Note on place names, foreign words, and pronunciations

In a trilingual country like Belgium, there are alternative words for almost everything, including place names. In general, I have used the names appropriate to the area of origin: i.e. Flemish names in Flanders and French names in Wallonia. Important exceptions are Bruges (should be Brugge), Antwerp (Antwerpen), and Brussels (Bruxelles/Brussel) which I have left in their familiar English forms. An extensive list of French–Flemish variants is given in the Glossary.

Foreign words appear in italics and pronunciations are in boldface. For example, "The Flemish use the word *voetpad*" and "Van Gogh was in fact **Van H!okh**".

— *Chapter One* —

WHAT IS BELGIUM?

Belgium is a miraculous compromise. Utterly artificial, it is a fusion of linguistically incompatible peoples thrust together by religio-historical chance, and sealed by a masterpiece of 19th century cartographic bravado. Over 2000 years ago, an ill-defined entity called Belgica had been spotted lurking at the violent northern edge of the Roman Empire. But thereafter no such thing as Belgium existed up until 1830. Once created, no one really expected the little nation to last out the decade. But survive it has, thanks to its remarkable capacity for compromise, practicality, and fudging: characteristics that still fundamentally shape the Belgian mindset.

Belgium can be roughly divided along linguistic lines. The northern half (Flanders or *Vlaanderen*) is a flat, richly agricultural land whose population mostly speak Flemish (*Vlaams*), a language very similar to the Dutch of neighboring Holland. The southern half (Wallonia or Wallonie) is mostly populated by speakers of French (*Français*) and various yokel French dialects known collectively as Walloon, though there are also small pockets of German-speaking people living around Eupen. To complete the picture, add Brussels, the historically Flemish, increasingly Francophone, nominally bilingual, and heartily multicultural "capital of Europe."

The very survival of Belgium relies on the compromise between its communities. As you will see, the regions and various factions in society are often openly antagonistic toward one another, but underneath all that, the people maintain a practical, "let's get on with it" spirit. This compromise is the essence of Belgian culture, along with a deadpan, self-effacing humor. While crises blow by and politicians wrangle, ordinary Belgians quietly tuck into some of Europe's finest food and best beer with a chuckle and a "so what" shrug.

PHYSICAL LANDSCAPE

There's no more evocative description of Belgian geography than Jacques Brel's poignantly bittersweet song—"Le Plat Pays"—or the flat country. Some typical lines include:

> "With the great North Sea, as the last empty space,
> Just the void of the dunes to arrest its advance...
> With a sky so low that a canal gets lost in it…
> With a sky of such grey that you have to forgive it…
> This flat country of mine."

Portraying a country that is at once dreary yet loveable, this is self-effacing Belgian modesty at its best. But one line's untranslatably poetic description of the country's "cathedrals as its only mountains"

"Look—an undulation!" Belgium isn't entirely flat.

doesn't apply to the whole nation. Well not quite. Northern Belgium is indeed home to the fertile, pan-flat, drained marshland of Flanders and some of Europe's widest expanses of sand along the North Sea coast. But the center of the country is decorated with plenty of gently

13

rolling contours. The relief climaxes in the heavily forested Ardennes "mountains" of the southeast, though the term "hills" would be much more appropriate. Even at their highest point, they only reach 694 meters (2277 feet) above sea level. This is the Signal de Botrange, an extremely undramatic minor incline, but one that still manages to draw local tourists on the few weekends a year when there's enough snow for a bit of skiing.

WEATHER

The weather has a crucial bearing on national character. In Belgium, the grey skies, low clouds, and drizzling rain seem to nourish the stoical national character of home-lovers. Of course, there can be days or even weeks of splendid summer sunshine accompanied by the buzzing of lawn mowers and hedge-cutters. But more memorable are the thick fogs in spring and autumn. Belgian winters are typically cold but not unbearable. You can expect two or three heavy snowfalls during a typical Brussels winter, after which the city looks briefly magnificent and the Brussels Ring road becomes even more of a death trap than normal. In the Ardennes, there is enough snow most years to serve the small ski runs, albeit briefly.

REGIONALISM

Since 1980, the kingdom of Belgium has existed as a federation of three regions: Wallonia, Flanders, and Brussels. The nation's two main regions, Wallonia and Flanders, are so autonomous that they occasionally appear to forget that they are part of a single, federal Belgium. "Flanders—at the heart of Europe" shouts a series of posters and advertisements trying to attract business and tourism to the region which gave the world many of the greatest painters during the Middle Ages. The regional identity of Wallonia is less defined and French-speakers are more likely than the Flemish to be proud of the sobriquet *Belgian*. Be careful of what you call them, however. Canadians are not American. Scots are not English. And Walloons are most self-consciously not French.

VITAL STATISTICS

Area	30,519 square kilometers (11,780 square miles)
Population	approximately 10.1 million
Language spoken	57% Flemish; 42% French; less than 1% German
Capital	Brussels
Relative wealth index	112.5 (taking a base rate for the EU as 100)
Average life-span	men 74.8 years; women 81.1 years Flemish people on average live 2.5 years longer than those in Wallonia.

Chapter Two

BELGIUM THROUGH TIME

These days, Belgian men might be stereotyped as tubby beer-drinkers living a quiet life and keeping their heads down. But in Roman times they were bloodthirsty warriors. *Asterix in Belgium* features fearless tribes of "brave Belgae"—and that's not supposed to be a sarcastic swipe. For several years around 50 B.C., a Belgian Asterix by the name of Ambiorix really did lead the Belgae tribe and proved a great nuisance to the Roman legions around Tongeren. "Of all the people of war, the Belgians are the bravest," Julius Caesar is supposed to have said. Of course Caesar's comments were aimed less at flattering the illiterate Belgian fighters and their chip-frying descendants than at explaining away a couple of unexpected, if short-term, military setbacks for the Roman legions. But today, the quote launches history lessons for Belgian school kids, much as Alfred's burnt cakes do for Brits.

THE LANGUAGE DIVIDE

The Belgae were a sizeable group of Gallo-Celtic warrior clans consisting of the Morini in Flanders, the Nervii in Brabant, the Atuatuci in Namur, the Eburones in Limburg, and several others, around half a million in total. They arrived in the 2nd century B.C. armed with iron weapons and equipped with sea-worthy boats. The clans developed forges to improve their iron work using coal from Hainaut, and the coins which they made are thought to have been traded as far afield as Greece.

In a protracted series of harsh battles between 57 and 52 B.C., the Romans conquered the Belgae—the Nervii were defeated near Cambrai and once the Atuatuci of Namur were crushed, the other clans surrendered. "Belgica" became a Roman province and the fertile plains of Wallonia proved suitable for agricultural development. But the Romans decided not to bother with the impenetrable forest and swamp of northern Belgium.

The area neglected by the Romans caught the fancy of Norse-Germanic Viking tribes who besieged the coasts with as many as 12 raids between A.D. 795 and 1098. By the 12th century, some of these tribes had decided to stay put and were comfortably settled in what is now Flanders.

Thus Flanders developed a Germanic language, while Wallonia separately adopted Romanic Latin, and eventually, French. Exactly what happened to the legendary Belgae tribe is not clearly recorded, but quite unwittingly they were to give their name to present-day Belgium some 19 centuries later.

EARLY UNREST

From the middle of the 3rd century A.D., the Roman Empire was reeling from a series of Gothic raids. At its northern flank, Belgica became increasingly dominated by the Germanic Franks. By the end of the 4th century, Tournai, once the most important town of the Roman Empire, started to develop into a Frankish royal city. Childeric I, the king of Gaul and father of Clovis, established his capital here while Charlemagne, the great Gallic empire builder, came from just across today's border at Aix-la-Chapelle (now Aachen, Germany). Charlemagne dragged Belgica into the French-Gallic empire, or, the Belgians might argue, dragged France into a greater Belgium. He is also known amongst Francophone kids for having "invented school," a "fact" celebrated in a well-known France Gall song.

From the end of Charlemagne's era (A.D. 814) even Flanders had theoretically become a vassal of the French. Flanders was still separated from Wallonia by thick forests, and remained largely autonomous; increasingly so as towns such as Bruges, Gent, and Ieper developed into bustling international trade and textile centers in the 13th century.

THE "LOW COUNTRIES"

The "Low Countries" region encompassing today's Belgium, Netherlands, and Luxembourg formed a patchwork of medieval duchies, counties, and principalities with shifting alliances that slowly coalesced under the leadership of the French dukes of Burgundy. The exact boundaries vary through history, but at times stretched as far as Lille, Gravelines, and Cambrai in today's France, notably including Artois, the district centered on Arras.

This was not a nation state—such a concept didn't appear in Europe until relatively recently. The French-speaking overlords simply administered a jigsaw of disconnected territorial fragments and expanded their rule by tactical marriages or conquest. Initially that hardly mattered. For the peasant majority, medieval life was simply a battle for day-to-day survival. So long as their traditions were not threatened, and taxes not increased, relatively few cared or even noticed who their rulers were (not so different from Belgium today, one might cynically venture).

As Flanders quietly developed into a major textile and trade center, more people moved into towns. By the 14th century, these towns had become some of the richest, best educated in Europe. And educated people do the unthinkable—question the divine rights of their feudal lords! Organized into guilds (somewhat like trade unions), the Flemish townsfolk were prepared to fight for civic liberties and privileges which set them apart from peasants. These tussles occasionally boiled over into full scale uprisings, as in 1302 when Bruges guildsmen refused to pay a new round of taxes. Pieter de Coninck led the townsfolk in rooting out Francophones by the administration of a very basic Flemish language test: bad pronunciation of the Flemish phrase "*schild en vriend*" ("shield and friend") was punished with the sword. The rebellion spread, and the French responded by sending in a dazzling army of heavily armored knights. But the warriors were tricked into the Groeninghekouter marsh near Kortrijk, and simply got stuck in the mud.

This "Battle of the Golden Spurs" was unthinkably humiliatingly for the noble knights whose defeat at the hands of mere commoners undermined their chivalric myth of natural superiority. The battle remains a tremendous emotional landmark for Flemish nationalists. Although the French were soon back in control, the towns did manage to assert their rights, symbolic recognition of which eventually came to be enshrined in the Joyeuses Entrées—ceremonial visits by the future monarch to every part of his realm. Even today, new monarchs present themselves to each town, as the present crown prince Philippe and his new wife Mathilde recently did in 1999.

BURGUNDIANS AND AUSTRIANS

Despite a nod to the French kings, local power in Belgium coalesced in the hands of the Dukes of Burgundy as the 14th and 15th centuries progressed. The Burgundians had held Flanders since 1384. With strong armed rule and Machiavellian political maneuvers that add a sarcastic twist to his popular name, Philip the Good (1419–1467) managed to piece together a large, virtually coherent domain on the edge of the French empire. Initially he made a cheeky alliance with England against his supposed French overlords, capturing Joan of Arc whom he handed to the English for a bonfire party. But once France had agreed to release Burgundy and Flanders from vassal status, Philip switched sides and fought beside France against his former English allies. Brabant, Limburg, and Antwerp were inherited, Namur was bought, and Hainaut (packaged since 1299 with Holland and Zeeland) was won by subterfuge giving Philip most of present-day Belgium. The main gap in his collection was Liège, a neutral, religious enclave that remained an independent Prince-Bishopric until 1794! Liège was finally taken by revolutionary France. (Read Walter Scott's *Quentin Durward* for more information.)

Philip also managed to tighten his grip on the prosperous new towns, reeling in hard won civic privileges but simultaneously improving their economic performance. By the time he married Isabella of Portugal, he was rich and powerful enough to indulge in his passion for reading and to become a major patron of the arts.

Philip's son, Charles the Bold, married the King of England's sister and set about a series of wars planning to build an ever bigger Burgundian duchy into a kingdom in its own right. When Charles was killed in battle, his daughter and heir apparent Mary was kidnapped by fed-up Flemish citizens and released only when she agreed to grant again the civic rights that had been eroded over previous decades. Mary went on to marry the Holy Roman Emperor, Maximillian who became sole ruler when Mary fell off her horse and died. Suddenly, the Low Countries became part of the vast Hapsburg empire, ruled initially from Austria. And later from Spain. And later still from Austria once again…

SPANISH RULE

Maximillian's grandson Charles V (Charles Quint/Kaiser Karel) was born in Gent in 1500. Arguably the greatest Belgian ever, he was certainly one of the most powerful men ever to rule in Europe. He reigned over vast inherited domains "on which the sun never set" including Austria (which he later gave to his brother), Burgundy, the Low Countries, the Holy Roman Empire, Spain, and Spain's fabulously wealthy American conquests.

With Bruges's fortunes fading following the silting of its river estuary, Charles V encouraged the growth of Antwerp which became one of the most important cities in the 16th century world. The Antwerp Beurs stock market opened in 1531 and was soon turning over around a million sterling pounds per day. Antwerp was also a cultural center for painters, writers, and thinkers. William Shakespeare studied here. It was a cosmopolitan community, a medieval Manhattan, the greatest trading port of the Western world.

Throughout the Low Countries, a high level of education and the development of new printing processes meant that locals were increasingly literate. For the first time, people could read the Bible for themselves. And this led to a wave of doubt that the often corrupt Catholic church was really following "God's Way." While Charles V became ever more focused on Spain, Lutheran and Calvinist Protestantism spread rapidly across northern Europe, despite the Edict of Blood which threatened the death sentence for heresy.

The first Belgian Protestants to be burnt at the stake were two Augustinian monks who were roasted in Antwerp in 1523. But the city soon realized that killing nonconformists was very bad for business. After all, many of the heretics were rich traders. This tolerance did not, however, sit too well with the staunchly Catholic monarchy. But initial attempts to introduce a Spanish-style inquisition were strenuously resisted by the towns, who considered that an infringement of their traditional civic rights. Sparks really started to fly once Charles abdicated in 1555.

Charles V's son, Phillip II was not a compromise-prone Belgian. He had been brought up in Spain with all the ruthless heretic-burning zeal of a good contemporary Hispanic. In the liberal-minded Low Countries, this was to prove a severe problem. When Phillip II succeeded his father in the 1556, he was a bit surprised to find that in the Low Countries, people didn't always do what they were told. It was the start of a major conflict. The Dutch didn't want to change their beliefs. But the Belgians were effectively coerced over the generations to accept Catholicism, a situation that has resulted in the nation's considerable Catholic majority today.

THE DUTCH REVOLTS

In 1566, an extraordinary fever of civilian outrage at the rigid and heavy taxing system imposed by the Spanish swept through the Low Countries. This uprising was ruthlessly put down by King Philip's commander, the Duke of Alva, a year later. Yet taxes had to be raised to fund the garrisons of Spanish troops who stayed on to keep the peace. This fed the public's discontent and a second revolt erupted on April Fool's Day in 1572. Failed grain harvests, plague, and an English trade boycott had generally made everyone more miserable than ever. Dutch rebels managed to capture large caches of armaments which the king had shipped to the coast for an abortive invasion of England. And Spain reacted cautiously. It was also carefully watching the Franco–Belgian border in case the Protestant Huguenot leaders in Paris should use the opportunity to strike east. After the Huguenot leaders were massacred en masse in France, support for the rebels collapsed. With the pressure reduced, Alva set about a vicious retribution in Belgium—his troops swiftly retook the region and sacked Mechelen to supplement their poor wages. But they failed to take Holland, where the leader of the rebels, William of Orange, had retreated. William was able to defend that area by opening the dykes and water courses and flooding low-lying fields so that Alva's men couldn't march across them.

The war became a stalemate. Again Spain was having trouble paying its troops and, in 1576, a mutiny of the unpaid Spanish garrison virtually destroyed Antwerp. In the Union of Arras in January 1579, many of the Belgian counties decided to cut their losses and say "sorry" to Spain, returning to Philip's empire. At the same time, however, the Dutch United Provinces declared themselves outside such jurisdiction in what might have been the world's first declaration of independence: the Union of Utrecht. Neither Dutch nor Spanish signatories would have realized at the time that they were setting the first stage in the eventual foundation of a new nation: the Netherlands. And that what was left would eventually be moulded into Belgium.

17TH CENTURY DECLINE

The Dutch revolts proved to be an unmitigated economic disaster for proto-Belgium. The primary concern of the Spanish regime was to re-Catholicize the population. Those Protestants who survived the reinforced inquisition under the Spanish fled to Holland or England, draining the land of many of its skilled workers. Flanders and Brabant, once at the forefront of Europe, were now forgotten provinces of a distant, conservative Hapsburg empire ruled from Spain (and later Austria). The once great city of Antwerp withered: 6% of its population had been massacred in the mutiny of 1576 and its trade role undermined by decades of war. Trade with the Indes, which brought in much revenue for Antwerp, moved steadily away to Amsterdam and Rotterdam, especially after 1580 when the Dutch started taking for themselves many of Portugal's colonies. The port of Antwerp was closed to legitimate international trade following the revolts. Many of the unemployed Flemish seamen turned to piracy in order to make ends meet.

What remained of artistic life in Belgium took a sharp turn toward the conservative. The sparkling intellectual world that had encouraged the humanitarian thinkers like Erasmus and Thomas More gave way to a retrograde obsession with religion. Artists like Rubens

23

thrived painting vast Italian-influenced Baroque canvases glorifying the daunting, overpowering Catholic mainstream. The opulence of his work was a deliberate contrast to the discredited austerity of Calvinism and to the horrific doomsday surrealism of Breughel, which had prevailed a few years previously. Rubens himself was saddened by the state of his once great Antwerp which he described as "languishing like a consumptive body" and, in between master-pieces, he acted as diplomat to try and improve relations between Spain and England in hope of a cure for the city. But to no avail. The war that had rumbled on between Catholic and Protestant Europe from the Dutch revolts lasted 80 years, and was finally concluded in the 1648 Peace of Westphalia (Peace of Münster). But this was anything but good for Antwerp. In a nod to the Dutch, the treaty closed the River Schelde to shipping and thereby killed off Antwerp's lifeblood, trade.

THE BRABANÇONNE REVOLUTION

Carlos (Charles) II the last Spanish Hapsburg emperor died childless in 1700. In his will, he left his realms to Philip d'Anjou, the grandson of the French king Louis XIV. Louis gleefully prepared to take control of the Spanish Netherlands (i.e. Belgium) but Holland and England were having none of it. A further expanded France would have been too much of a threat and the affair sparked off the War of Spanish Succession. For a decade or so, the English Duke of Marlborough skirmished with French troops across Belgium with key battles at Tienen, Ramillies, Oudenaarde, and Malplaquet. Finally, in 1713, France reluctantly signed the Treaty of Utrecht which gave Belgium to the Austrian Hapsburg empire.

By the late 18th century, the artificial division between Dutch and Flemish cultures had solidified into real differences. Although later Austrian rulers proved relatively enlightened, Emperor Joseph II, a reformist, nearly caused a war with Holland when he tried to re-open Antwerp to international trade. His liberal attempts to legalize Protestant forms of worship were not only futile (by this stage there was barely a Protestant left in Belgium to welcome the move) but actually resulted in the 1789 rebellion referred to today as the Brabançonne Revolution. The "Revolution" led briefly to the creation of the independent United Belgian States and is still celebrated in the Belgian national anthem. However, this new independence was crushed within a year by the Austrian Hapsburgs.

THE FRENCH BARGE IN

The Austrians didn't last long. In 1792, at the battle of Jemappes, they were defeated by a French revolutionary army led by General Dumouriez. By 1794 the French had taken control of the whole region. The main result was the desecration and dispossession of the abbeys, in line with the anti-religious beliefs of the revolutionaries.

By 1799, Napoleon had come to power. He demanded that the Dutch allow an end to the blockade of the River Schelde. This was to allow the renovation of the port of Antwerp, which he described as a "pistol pointed at the heart of Britain". But Napoleon never got to fire that pistol. After the French attack on Russia and their subsequent ignominious retreat from Moscow in 1812, the Low Countries were once more in revolt. Napoleon's last-ditch attempt at a comeback in 1815 was a remarkable feat of mobilization considering he'd been in exile a few month earlier. However, his reign came to a definitive end when he was famously caught somewhat by surprise by Wellington's multinational armies at Waterloo, just south of Brussels.

DUTCH RULE

In 1815, the kingdom of the Netherlands was created by the Congress of Vienna in the aftermath of Waterloo. The Netherlands was a buffer state that lumped together the former United Provinces (today's Netherlands) and the Austrian Netherlands (today's Belgium). The new king William I declared Dutch the official language and set out to secularize the schools. This did not go down well at all with the

French-speaking population in the south. In July 1830, revolutionary fervor was again rising in France, and Brussels caught the wave a month later. One of history's most unlikely rebellions began as high-spirited concert-goers poured out of a performance of Auber's opera *La Muette de Portici* singing along to the patriotic aria "Amour Sacré de la Patrie" ("Sacred Love of Patriotism"). Given the circumstance, the Dutch did not recognize the rebellion, thinking it a joke. The troops stayed in their barracks. But before they knew it, the rebellion was spiralling out of control across the country.

Much to their bemusement, the Belgians suddenly found themselves with their very own state. A republican national constitution was rapidly formulated. But by the conservative norms of the day it seemed dangerously liberal. To give it a suitable veneer of respectability, the authors decided to graft on a figurehead monarchy. The kingdom of Belgium was born.

INDEPENDENCE: AN INAUSPICIOUS START

Scouts went fishing around the courts of Europe for a suitable king. After a few rejections, they settled for the pompous Leopold Saxe-Coburg as a politically appropriate (i.e. non-French, non-Dutch) compromise. Leopold had been "unemployed" since the untimely death of his wife Princess Charlotte, heir apparent of England. Having lost his hopes of becoming British consort and still keen to start a dynasty, he'd already been shopping for thrones around Europe. Having rejected Greece as a bit too risky, he finally decided to make the best of it with Belgium. Quite a feat at first, as the country was considered a joke by most outsiders. Talleyrand, the French statesman and diplomat, had gone so far as to say, "There are no Belgians, never have been any, never will be any." But Leopold was single-mindedly determined to give it a go despite the country's distinct lack of national spirit. Belgium's survival was threatened a year later by Dutch invasion, and by many subsequent attempts of foreign powers to divide it. But through careful maneuvering, Leopold maintained his fiefdom and by 1848, Belgium was strong enough to survive at a time when the majority of the European monarchies were tumbling or being shaken by revolutions.

INDUSTRIALIZATION AND GROWTH

Leopold's unexpected success was helped by his careful maintenance of political neutrality, and by the gradual industrialization of Wallonia. The economy took off mainly because of the equally unlikely success of his son Leopold II who, with Machiavellian cunning, managed to obtain sponsorship for his private venture to colonize the Congo. Initially dressed up as a humanitarian ideal, the Congo enterprise was soon revealed to be unmitigatedly exploitative. Leopold gained vast personal wealth from the agricultural and mineral resources at the expense of the colony's humanitarian rights. In 1908, a shamed Belgian government took over Leopold's Congo to repair the nation's dreadful reputation for colonial cruelty, which must have been particularly appalling given the callous norms of the day. But by this stage Leopold II had invested large sums of money in the development of Belgium. Brussels, in particular, was transformed from a relatively humble provincial town into a grand, fashionable Art Nouveau metropolis.

WAR

All progress came grinding to a halt in World War I. German troops poured across the border assuming that Belgium, being a neutral party, would not put up a fight. Though quickly overwhelmed, the plucky Belgians skirmished valiantly under their "Soldier King" Albert, who equally valiantly insisted on participating in the frontline action. They managed to hold out just long enough to allow the Allies to shore up the western front. The fields of Flanders became a mousse of blood and mud and the historic town of Ieper (since rebuilt) was pounded to ruins. Nonetheless, Albert refused to leave Belgian soil. Using a trick from the Dutch Revolt, he positioned his troops at De

27

Panne in far western Flanders, then blew holes in the dykes between his position and that of the advancing Germans. The intervening area was flooded and remained impassable for the rest of the war.

Belgium had an even harder time in World War II. Heavily bombed by both sides the country was invaded by Nazi Germany which not only decimated the Jewish community but also fomented tensions between the Francophone and the previously marginalized Flemish-speaking population. (See Chapter Four). King Leopold III proved much less statesmanlike than Albert I in World War I. Publicly suspected of collaborating, he was finally forced to abdicate in 1950.

RECENT HISTORY

Postwar Belgium has quietly done a very good job of making itself prosperous again, despite constantly teetering on the edge of a breakup along linguistic lines. Since 1963, the linguistic communities of the French, Flemish, and German speakers have been officially recognized. Belgium was also divided into regions in 1980 and has been a federal state since 1993, but it is still Belgium. Despite grave recessions in the heavy industries of Wallonia, the economy remains reasonably vibrant, thanks in part to the numerous international organizations which are based here—notably the Supreme Headquarters Allied Powers Europe (SHAPE) in Mons and NATO (since 1977) plus the gargantuan EU bureaucracy in Brussels.

BROAD-STROKES HISTORICAL ERAS

Belgae	from approximately 1500 B.C.
Roman	52 B.C.
Frankish	A.D. 5th century
Norse-Germanic Vikings	A.D. 9th century
Flemish golden era	A.D. 12th century
under nominal French suzerainty	
Battle of the Golden Spurs	A.D. 1302
Burgundian dynasty	A.D. 1419

Spanish/Hapsburg rule	A.D. 1482
Spread of Protestantism	A.D. 1520s
Dutch revolts	A.D. 1560s
Split with Netherlands	A.D. 1579
Austrian rule	A.D. 1701–1789
ejected by the Brabançonne Revolution	A.D. 1790–1792
French rule	A.D. 1795
Dutch rule	A.D. 1814
Independence	A.D. 1830
World War I	A.D. 1914–1918
World War II	A.D. 1939–1945

— *Chapter Three* —

GOVERNMENT
AND POLITICS

Politically Belgium is extremely fragmented. Every village and urban community (commune/*gemeente*) has an elected mayor and falls within one of three political regions (each with its own government). Simultaneously, communes also fall within separate linguistic communities (also with their own ministers). Overseeing all this is a federal government and a figurehead constitutional monarch. Political parties divide linguistically *and* by class (Catholic, liberal, and socialist) and issue (Greens, nationalists, etc.). It's mind-bogglingly complex. Yet somehow, everyone manages to compromise just enough to form workable governing coalitions. How very Belgian.

THE MONARCHY

The head of state is a constitutional monarch. At present, the throne is filled by the jolly King Albert II, who is expected to hand over his duties to his son Philippe before long, now that Phil has at last found himself a suitable wife.

The Kings So Far

> "King Zahir Sha (of 1960s Afghanistan), like the king of the Belgians in his country, was the only power able to calm the game between the different, turbulent ethnicities..."

So said Jacques Gourguechon in his *Voyage au Pamir*. And we've seen what happened to Afghanistan once they lost their king! So far, Belgium remains a constitutional kingdom. In a 1999 opinion poll, 70% of Belgians thought that their country would have split without the monarchy. But with a popular new princess for the millennium, the royal line looks set to continue.

As in any country, the popularity of the monarchy has fluctuated wildly with individual personalities and press attitudes to them. The first two kings, Leopold I and II, were hardly anybody's first-choice candidates but brought the country riches. Warrior king Albert I, whose helmeted statue adorns most Belgian towns, was well-loved for his World War I efforts. He died in a tragic accident while rock-climbing near Dinant, to great national consternation.

Leopold III's record in World War II proved his undoing. He stayed in German-occupied Belgium for much of the war and was initially perceived as a lonely, prisoner figure. But public sympathy evaporated when, after his wife Queen Astrid died in a car crash, Leopold seemed over-hasty in remarrying. What exactly was his ambiguous relationship with the Nazis? Captured or collaborating? What about the birthday greeting he sent Hitler? Toward the end of the war, Leopold was moved to Austria by the retreating Germans and temporarily replaced by his brother Charles as regent. On his return,

31

he was virtually forced to hand over the throne to his son Baudouin, to avoid the abolition of the monarchy once and for all.

Baudouin is usually remembered as irreproachably good, if a teeny bit dull. Locals suspect that he would have preferred to have been a priest than a king. Distant but fatherly and overwhelmingly respected, he and the national football team managed to keep the country together against an increasingly acrimonious squabble among the linguistic communities in the 1970s and 1980s. Baudouin gained further respect over his handling of the 1990 abortion legalization bill. This was a law which his Catholic conscience would not allow him to approve, but which, as the leader of a modern European nation, he felt he could not impede either. So, in a very Belgian compromise, he abdicated for the day, leaving his brother to sign it.

Baudouin's early death in 1993 caused a shock wave on a scale similar to the mass hysteria following the death of Princess Di. Many Belgians have admitted to crying on hearing the news. The funeral was a moment of national reflection and caused a rare upwelling of Belgian national togetherness as Flemings and Walloons stood together amidst the flowers strewn on the grounds of the royal palace.

The present king, Albert II, is the brother of the childless Baudouin. He is well-liked, notwithstanding the salacious revelation that a London-based papier-mâché sculptress by the name of Delphine Boël is in fact Albert's illegitimate love child. While the news caused great interest amongst the gossip-loving public, there was no hint of a popularity backlash. It is well-known that during much of the 1970s and 1980s, Albert and his wife Paola led different lives. This was never considered consequential as it had always been assumed that Albert's son Philippe would take over rather than his father. But Baudouin's early death caught Phillipe as yet unmarried, and a reluctant Albert took on the job to give his son a little more wooing time. Phillipe appears to have managed with a degree of success that few expected in finding, marrying, and rapidly impregnating the radiant Mathilde d'Udekem d'Acoz.

Present Attitudes to the Monarchy

There's a general feeling that Francophones are more pro-monarchist than the Flemish, many of whom reportedly see the monarchy as an anachronism, meaningless within a unified Europe. But both the Flemish and the Francophones seem to prefer the idea of a king to that of an elected president. And both communities were evenly split on the question of whether the approximately 400,000,000BEF annual cost of supporting the monarchy is worth the money (0.17% of tax revenues).

Other Belgian Royals

Impress your Belgian friends with your knowledge of the lesser members of the royal clan. For example, there are two queens (Fabiola, widow of Baudouin, and Paola). Or that should Philippe suddenly disappear, it would be his sister, Princess Astrid, that becomes queen, rather than Philippe's brother Laurent.

The "male takes precedence rule" that still stands in the U.K. was dropped in Belgium in favor of a strict age order. A breakthrough for women's equality? Perhaps. But some Belgian jokers claim that it was more a case of averting the "worrying possibility" that chubby Prince Laurent could become king. Although Laurent is a better public speaker than most of his family, his penchant for surrounding himself with fast cars and beauty queens doesn't create a regal image. Nor does his friendship with Princess Stephanie of Monaco, considered a "royal bimbo." Although quietly admired for not giving a damn, Laurent is harshly teased as the family dunce. There was long debate amongst the public over a military parade in which Laurent, against all protocol, saluted the army dogs. Was it because he didn't know better, because he hadn't learnt the rules, or that he's an animal lover?

Hidden away at the château at Argenteuil, up a forest track reached by a perilously dangerous turn off the Brussels Ring, Princess Lilian de Réthy, the second wife of Leopold III still ekes out an existence on her meagre 15.4 million BEF government pension.

Marie José, daughter of Belgian king Albert I became queen of Italy on May 6, 1946 when her husband Prince Umberto took over from his discredited father King Victor Emmanuel. Just her luck. A month later the Italian monarchy was abolished. She now lives fairly incognito in Switzerland.

King Baudouin's sister Joséphine-Charlotte lives the Belgian dream. She got herself a Luxembourg address by marrying Prince Jean in 1953. They're now Grand Duke and Duchess.

THE FEDERAL GOVERNMENT

On paper, the Belgian king has greater power than most of Europe's constitutional monarchs. But in reality, he rarely uses his authority. Much more power lies with the Federal Parliament (Federale Kamers/Chambres Fédérales). This is divided into two parliamentary houses nominally similar to those in the United States. The Senate (Senaat/Sénat) has 71 members, 40 of which are elected by the people every four years. Once elected, they get to choose the other 31 members.

The House of Representatives (Kamer van Volksvertegen-woordigers/Chambre des Représentants) is elected entirely by the people, also on a four-year cycle. The Prime Minister is found from this house once a coalition of parties has hammered out a working relationship, generally from the best-represented party. There are 18 ministers at national level including the Prime Minister and the Secretaries of State. In addition there are special government commissioners charged with sorting out pressing issues of the day: at present working on food safety, metropolitan policy (read unemployment), and "administrative simplification."

There is a bewildering choice of political parties. Parties represented in the federal parliament since the 1999 elections include the following in approximate order of seats won:

VLD   *Vlaamse Liberalen en Democraten*
                   Flemish Liberals and Democrats

CVP *Christelijke Volkspartij*
Christian People's Party (Flemish)

PS *PartiSocialiste*
Francophone Socialist Party

Vlaams *Vlaams Blok*
Blok Flemish Nationalists

SP (SPA) *Socialistische Partij (Anders)*
Flemish Socialist party, renamed Aug 2001

PSC *Parti Social Chrétien*
Francophone Christian Democrats

Ecolo *Ecolo*
Green party (Francophone)

Agalev *Agalev*
Green party (Flemish)

PRL *Parti Réformateur Libéral*
Liberal Reformists with FDR/MCC

FDF *Front Démocratique des Francophones*
Democratic Front (stridently Francophone)

MCC *Mouvement des Citoyens pour le Changement*
Citizens Movement for Change

VU-VVD *Volksunie/Vlaamse Vrije Democraten*
People's Union/Free democrats

ID21   *ID21*
            A liberal–social party with VU-VVD

The average voter tends to divide the parties along linguistic lines and then look for political pigeonholes: Catholic (PSC and CVP which ruled for most of the 1990s), liberal (VLD, PRL, FDF, and MCC), or socialist (SP/SPA and PS), although the Greens (Agalev or Ecolo) are a growing force, and, since 1999, were included in the ruling coalition for the first time.

As only parties gaining above a minimum threshold of the vote get to take seats in the house, electoral blocks are formed between some smaller parties so that together they may have the necessary momentum. Hence the mainly Flemish VU-VVD-ID21 group themselves as a single election fighting team, as do the Francophone FDF-PRL-MCC block. Smaller parties which fail to form such blocks include the Vivant party whose 2% proved insufficient to get a single deputy in the house of representatives. Compare this with the PSC whose 5.9% gave them 10 seats.

There has been a disquieting rise in the electoral popularity of the far right parties. Most notably the Vlaams Blok which is now the largest party in Antwerp, but also the xenophobic National Front (which remains unrepresented despite winning 1.5% of the vote in 1999). Nonetheless, these results should not necessarily be construed as a sign of rising fascism within Belgium. It's more as a sign that the people are fed up with a political status quo where nothing seems to get done.

If anyone wanted to, they could look more closely at the policies of the Belgian political parties who post their manifestos, publications, and latest initiatives on the internet (accessed via the general website http://www.politicalresources.net/belgium.htm). But on the whole, people seem happier just grumbling and forgetting all about politics. Most Belgians vote, but only because it's a legal obligation: those who don't vote are fined.

REGIONS AND COMMUNITIES

In 1963, the country's linguistic divisions were marked out creating three linguistic communities. The Flemish, Francophone, and Germanophone communities now each have their own government ministers led by a "minister president." Then regionalization in 1980 officially created the Flemish and Walloon regions. As of 1994, these divisions crystallized into today's federal system with regional parliaments for Flanders, Wallonia, and the Brussels-Capital regions. These also have their own ministers and minister-presidents. While the government for Flanders and for the Flemish community is effectively the same, the Wallonia government is altogether different from that of the French community. But I've yet to meet a local who fully understands where the difference lies in the roles of the two sets of governments! And things are unlikely to be any clearer after the constitutional revisions of 2001.

PROVINCES AND ARRONDISSEMENTS

Until federalization, Belgium consisted of nine provinces loosely based on the ancient feudal duchies and counties. Four of these (Hainaut, Namur, Liège, and Luxembourg) now form the bulk of Francophone Wallonia. Four more (Limburg, Antwerp, and East and West Flanders) make up most of Flanders. Brabant, the multilingual ninth province with Brussels at its heart, was split in the mid-1990s. Vlaams Brabant Province was added to the Flanders region, and Brabant Wallon to Wallonia, leaving Brussels-Capital as a third region rather than a province. Each of the now 10 provinces are further subdivided into around half a dozen administrative arrondissements.

THE COMMUNE/GEMEENTE

The commune is the smallest organizational unit, whether it be a village, or the equivalent of a city borough. In Belgium, the commune has much authority—it runs the schools and issues such hallowed

37

documents as driver's licenses and passports (until 2001). Belgium has 589 communes, 19 in Brussels alone, many of which have particularly grand town halls (Maison Communale/Gemeenthuis).

The local layer of power lies at the commune level where a *bourgmestre/burgemeester* (mayor) has a surprising level of importance and power in comparison to the town or district councils in the U.K. Mayors make self-conscious attempts to associate themselves with any event or promotion in the commune.

BELGIUM—IS IT ABOUT TO SPLIT?

Unity, (or disunity) is a constant issue in Belgium. Daniel de Bruycker described his Belgium as "the only country that wonders if it even exists". There are occasional waves of intercommunal handholding —like on the death of King Baudouin or in the wake of the terrible pedophile cases in the late 1990s (See Chapter Six). But like in Canada, the spectre of a possible separation is always there, waved like a bully's club by nationalist groups to get political concessions.

Flemish Nationalism

Flanders was an economic powerhouse in the 15th century, and one of the richest areas of Europe. By the 19th century, it had lost chunks to the Netherlands and France and had become something of an agricultural backwater. With the development of the new state of Belgium, the upper echelons of Flemish society took to speaking French, possibly due to the backlash against the imposition of *Nederlands* during Dutch rule. French was the language of power spoken by the nobility, by government institutions, the army, secondary schools, universities, and even the law courts. However, the more plebeian Flemings became relegated by language to virtually second-class citizens.

The increasing use of French had dire consequences. In World War I, Flemish soldiers were executed for not obeying the orders of Francophone officers because they couldn't understand what had been said. And court cases were often heard but not understood by the main actors themselves. The Flemish literary movement, championed by writers like Guido Gezelle in the 19th century, steadily became more politicized after World War I. Standing up for the non-French speakers in Belgium, the Flemish national movement styled themselves after Christian pacifists. Keen to avoid conflict and aware of the possible gains, Flemish Nationalist groups collaborated heavily with invading Germans during World War II . This proved initially effective but, in actuality, masked the divide-and-rule motive the Germans had in mind. The "liberators" rapidly lost their appeal. But the damage was done. The Flemish nationalist movement became tarnished with its pro-Nazi image. Politically sidelined from the socio-democratic mainstream, it became something of an embarrassment to liberal Flemings.

Today, the linguistic communities enjoy equal language rights. Flanders has a great deal of autonomy in the present federal structure, and once the stumbling block to the country's prosperity, Flanders is now the economically more dynamic half of the country. But the nationalist cause has not died. Founded in 1977, the right-wing Vlaams Blok nationalist political group has recently been gathering an ever-increasing slice of the vote. And in what sounds like a comical farce, but is actually a serious political statement, large numbers of Flemings gather once a year to cycle around the periphery of Brussels. This event is known as De Gordel (The Girdle), and is a symbolic reminder that Brussels is surrounded. By Flanders.

Walloon Nationalism

Don't expect to hear about it! Admittedly during the 1950s, it was the French-speaking community which was on the verge of insurrection over the Royal Question. But there is no equivalent nationalist movement in the Francophone half of Belgium and the nearest you'll find to extremists are the handful of spoilsports who occasionally throw thumbtacks on the route of De Gordel to puncture Flemish tires.

Even if independence made economic sense, an independent Wallonia would probably remain unpopular. For most Walloons the French are more despised than the Flemish. And an isolated Wallonia might end up as a mere forgotten adjunct to France. Visit somewhere like Roubaix near Lille to picture the nightmarish scenario. Most Walloons simply scoff at any talk of nationalism: "We're Belgians and that's it."

Communes with Secondary Language Rights

On a day-to-day level, Flanders and Wallonia effectively operate as entirely separate countries. Each has its own TV network, its own political parties and parliament, its own newspapers, etc. In fact, a Walloon hears more about France than about Flanders; and a Fleming, more about anywhere in the world other than about Wallonia. But on the periphery of Brussels, there are a few special flash points. Six communes which are politically within Flanders have relatively large populations (even majorities) of Francophones. These communes were granted *à facilité* language rights in the 1960s, i.e. the recognition that much of the community was Francophone and "needed time to learn Flemish". It is here that intercommunal friction tends to flare. From the Flemish point of view, it's incomprehensible why even after several decades, so few Francophones have learnt the official language of the commune. And the Flemish feel humiliated at not being able to use their own language in the daily transactions conducted in their own towns. Francophones argue that many French communes are equally swamped with non-Francophones (mainly non-Belgians) and that, anyway, it goes against the grain of democracy to force the majority of a population to speak a minority language.

At least one commune tried to introduce a Flemish language examination, which residents had to pass before buying and owning land in the town. This, however, broke EU guidelines on discrimination. The controversial Peeters Circular in the late 1990s brought this issue to a head again. It pointed out that all residents had had enough time to learn Flemish by now and should start receiving all official communication in Flemish. This has since been ruled out too but the issue caused plenty of bad blood. To this day, tension plagues the flash point communities. Francophone friends in Overijse have had their doorsteps paint-bombed and have found that letters addressed in French occasionally go astray. Tak Aktie Komitee (TAK) radicals have been accused of jamming up the locks of Francophone schools in flash point communities with glue.

— Chapter Four —

LANGUAGE

Belgium is officially trilingual. French and Flemish are the main languages, while German is spoken as a mother tongue by a mere 68,000 nationals in the far east of the country around Eupen. Even this three-way split is an over-simplification. There are several sub-dialects of Flemish and a variety of almost mutually unintelligible Walloon languages, only loosely based on French. And in the capital there's the unique "cockneyesque" Bruxellois dialect, spoken in the small Marolles area.

MULTILINGUAL BELGIANS

Belgians have a remarkable linguistic ability. In many jobs, the ability to speak multiple languages is considered a prerequisite. In an extreme case, I know of a 16-year-old lad who was refused a part-time job at McDonalds because he was "only" bilingual—they wanted French, Flemish, and English from their burger salesmen. Some Brussels communes are short of policemen because the candidates flunk their language examinations. Secretarial job postings in Euroland may ask for two other languages, possibly Russian and Turkish, in addition to English and French or Flemish.

The relative abundance of English speakers is a double-edged sword for long-term visitors. Speak bad French in a shop in Paris and the attendant may just tut and wander off elsewhere. But at least you'll have an incentive to improve your French. In Brussels the shop assistant will probably hear your accent and reply in English. You'll almost always find someone who'll understand you in Belgium, so it is not entirely necessary to learn the language(s) in order to survive. However, without at least one local language, escaping the expatriate circus and delving into the real culture will prove pretty much impossible.

Why Do They Speak English so Well?

There are several theories. Generally, the Flemish seem more fluent than the Francophones, a fact put down to the more limiting nature of a "small" language and, more likely to the constant exposure to English on TV. The Flemish/Dutch market is apparently too small to justify dubbing TV shows. So when they sit glued to *The Simpsons*, Flemish kids are actually learning English. Francophones have the mixed blessing of pre-dubbed films aimed at the bigger French market, though in many cases movies are offered in a choice of versions: dubbed or in *Version Originale* (VO) i.e. subtitled.

English can at times be a diplomatic compromise in the French–Flemish linguistic war. Rather than speak each other's language, why not find some neutral ground? I know locals who would speak English when they are visiting pubs in Leuven or Gent if that saves them admitting to being French-speaking Belgians. These compromises also make economic sense for businesses in bilingual areas or for pan-Belgian advertising slogans; using English saves the awkward decision of which language to place above the other.

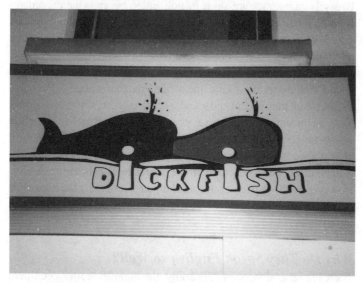

Many locals speak excellent English, but are not always aware of the funnier nuances, as you can see from the sign at this fishmonger's shop!

Flemish and Nederlands

Flemish (*Vlaams*) is essentially a localized form of Dutch. At school, Flemish kids learn to read and write in *Nederlands* (the official name for the Dutch language). But between *Vlaams* and *Nederlands*, there are many differences in vocabulary and some in structure and expression. Differences are distinctive enough that *Nederlands*-speakers are unlikely to confuse a Dutchman and a Belgian.

Flemish Dialects

Linguists once analyzed the Flemish language into five main dialect groups, each subdivided into half a dozen sub-languages. Fortunately, many of these are only spoken within the Netherlands, and a mere dozen or so in Belgium. From 1893 to the 1960s, efforts were made to overcome this regionalism and create a standardized, officially "correct" Flemish language. The result was not to everyone's taste: some considered it a sort of Flemish Esperanto. "*Verkaveling-svlaams*," it was wittily dubbed by journalist Geert Van Istendael (a *verkaveling* being a characterless suburban housing development).

In reality, the old dialects continue to heavily affect the sound of Flemish spoken in the regions, from the languorous sloth of the Limburg accent to the "sh-sh-shluring" sounds that give Aalst a reputation for producing the ugliest accent in Flanders. In Aalst dialect, Aalst is pronounced **Olsht**.

The most notable differences between *Nederlands* and standard Flemish show up in cases when a word of French extraction is used. Typically, Flemish tries to be more Dutch than the Dutch, and will create a word while Dutch–*Nederlands*-speakers would adopt the French word into their language. Thus, the Dutch call a spin-drier a *centrifuge* while the Flemish use the term *droogzwierder*. A sidewalk or pavement in Dutch is the same as the French word *trottoir*, but the Flemish use the word *voetpad*.

Flemish and Dutch Pronunciation

Flemish–Dutch transliteration is pretty systematic, but the pronunciations are rather different from those an English speaker anticipates.

Vowels

Watch especially for double-letter vowels which suggest a lengthening rather than an alteration of the single-letter sound. Logically, this is eminently more systematic than in English and offers the bonus effect of keeping most Francophones and Anglophones hopelessly confused.

The *e* in Flemish is pronounced like the **e** in the English word *met* while *ee* sounds like the **a** in *mate*. The English **ee** sound is denoted by a Flemish/Dutch *i*.

45

O is pronounced like the **o** in *mop* while **oo** in Flemish sounds like the **o** in *mope*. A long English **oo** as in *moon* might be transliterated with an *oe* in Dutch, although the sound is a little less rounded. A more rounded English **oo**, or German *ü* would be closer to a Dutch *u* or *uu*.

Ij is effectively a single-letter vowel pronounced somewhere between the vowel sound in *my* and the **ay** in *may*. Important for *ijs* (ice or ice cream).

Ui is pronounced like **oh** said by a sneering upper-class toff attempting a Peter Sellers' mock French accent.

Consonants

G is pronounced rather like a throaty **h!** as many football fans will have gathered thanks to the fame of Ruud Gullit (**Rude H!oollit**). Van Gogh was in fact **Van H!okh**. *J* is pronounced **y** rather like in German. Good luck with *ch*, which is a raspy **kh** sound.

Eye-catching Flemish Details

Putting *'t* in front of a Noun

This is not a crude attempt of Flemings to pretend that they're from Yorkshire, although the *'t* does serve a similar grammatical purpose; it denotes *the* (short for *het*, the neuter definite article).

Some nationalists have suggested that referring to the Flemish Lion (the national symbol) as *Het Leeuw* (neuter) would set it immediately apart from any less patriotic *De Leeuw* (masculine) that one might see in Antwerp's zoo.

The *tje* Suffix

This suffix added to the end of a name or word suggests little. This can be cute and friendly when said between friends. But it might be fighting talk between two burly lumberjacks.

French French versus Belgian French

Standard Belgian French is not quite the same as French spoken in France, although the difference is no greater than that between American and British English.

As a Brit, I had never heard anyone use the greetings "Hello bloke" or "pip pip" until I went to the United States. There, waggish Americans seemed to consider both turns of phrase examples of archetypal English. The French French seem to have a similar misconception that Belgians plonk the phrase *une fois* at the end of every other sentence. In the Belgium I know, the only time you're likely to hear this is in a signalled self-mimicking comedy sketch. However, there are some very real ways in which Belgian French does vary from that of France itself.

Numbers

The French French count some of their numbers in base 20. Thus 96 is *quatre-vingt seize* (4x20+16). As far as I know it's the only European language to do so with the exception of Kartuli (the language of ex-Soviet Georgia). The practical Belgians have no truck with such oddities. Francophone Belgians call 70 *septante* rather than *soixante–dix*, and 90 *nonante* rather than *quatre vingt dix*. This is a common-sense solution that French French snobbishly deride, much in the way that priggishly self-righteous Brits can't abide spelling *colour* as *color* in the common-sense American fashion. Strangely, Belgian French does, however, keep the term *quatre-vingt* (4x20) for 80. Perhaps this is to prove that they too are capable of a little Latin idiosyncrasy. Or that they're not Swiss.

Le Lunch

Francophone Belgians suffer less from the terrors of Anglicized terminology (commonly nicknamed *Franglais*) than their Gallic cousins and there's no Belgian language police to prevent the spread of "*le* job," "*le* weekend," or "*le* board-meeting." Belgians are not self-conscious in avoiding "*le* stress" by sitting down to "*un bon lunch*," which is likely to be very *bon* indeed.

Mr Hillier—He Acted Too Familiar

If you speak French you'll realize that *tu* and *vous* both mean *you*. But deciding which of the two terms to use in conversation is a diplomatic minefield. The standard rule is to use *tu* when speaking to children, family, and close friends, and *vous* to pretty much anyone else you meet, unless the older of you gallantly suggests a switch to a friendlier *tu*. Using *vous* with a lover suggests you're angry with him or her. Using *tu* with your boss is downright insolent. At least that is the rule of thumb in France.

Belgians are noticeably quicker to switch to *tu*, and thus tend to think of the French as cold or arrogant. Meanwhile, the French see the Belgians as over-familiar. Watch the discomfort that results. Incidentally, inappropriate *tu* familiarity is accepted from foreigners—Moroccan and Turkish shopkeepers, particularly—whose total disdain of the *vous* is usually taken to be quaint and endearing rather than insulting. Note that in contrast, *vous* is used in some Walloon dialects in virtually any case without any implied formality. Indeed, my wife's aged Walloon aunt used to address her own mother as *vous* and still uses the term to address her sister.

Belgian French Pronunciation

As in any country, there are numerous regional differences in accents which make for easy jokes amongst the locals. Belgian French accents that gargle exaggeratedly throaty sounds where textbook French has none—e.g. *graaf* for *grave* (bad)—is considered lower class. A hard **kh** sound is thrown gratuitously into innocent words like *mon cher* (my dear) which becomes more like *mo' shairkh*.

Exactly where thick accent blends into Walloon dialect remains a blurred line. The nasal *nin* (not) used by some people instead of the correct French *pas* is more than a pronunciational difference. But it is likely to be understood locally and is handy if you want to imitate the dull, flat Namur twang for deadpan comic effect.

Using French Computers

Francophone Belgian computer users often prefer to use the English operating system than the French one. Not surprising when a simple term like font is rendered as the awkward mouthful: *police de caractères*.

Touch-typists are in for a shock if the keyboard has been designed for French-speaking users. While most of the keys seem to be in place, the Q and A keys have been swapped, as have Z and W. This so-called "AZERTY" format also forces you to use the shift/upper case keys for numbers and full stops. This is to provide keys for accented letters, so typing what you'd expect to be 27.90 comes out as éè;çà.

Translated Sayings

There are hundreds of proverbs and sayings in any language. Here are a few from Flemish and French:

For next to nothing/for peanuts
For an apple and an egg (Flemish)
For a mouthful of bread (French)

You can't have your cake and eat it
You can't have the butter and the money of the butter (French)

I won't beat about the bush
I won't take four routes to get there (French)

I'm drunk
I'm farty (French)

It's nowhere near ready
It's not near the door (Flemish)

Walloon

"*Mô m'tièsse*": My head aches (*mô* = bad, m'= my, *tièsse* (or *tchess*) = head). And so it does when I try to take in all the swirling varieties of Walloon dialect. Walloon is based on French but only in the most tenuous of fashions. And to talk of Walloon in the singular is barely appropriate—it can be subdivided into several dialects that barely resemble one another.

For example, in standard French, watch out is *attention*. In some Walloon dialects it's very similar: *atincion*. In Liège, a possible alternative is *astème*. In Binche, you could shout *"arwête!"*

While older people still speak Walloon, it is not taught in school. Although Walloon is mostly an oral language, there have been plays written in Walloon, and the Assimil series publishes a pocket Walloon phrase book with words in the Charleroi, Namur, and Liège sub-dialects. Visit http://ourworld.compuserve.com/homepage/roger_thijs/langbel.htm for examples of many Walloon and of Flemish dialects.

Bruxellois

The language of old Brussels is an entertaining mix of French and Flemish, with odd words of Spanish and Hebrew extraction thrown in. Some streets signs in the Marolles district now have trilingual road signs—French, Flemish, and Bruxellois. The difference is not always minor, e.g. Rue du Faucon (in French) = Valkstraat (in Flemish) = de Builestroet (in Bruxellois).

Toone, the capital's last traditional puppet theater, used to do shows in Bruxellois but the curator José Géal recently told *The Bulletin* that such shows are increasingly few and far between because "nobody speaks it any more". If you want to, you can still rent video tapes of two classic Bruxellois plays, *Bosmans et Coppenole* and *Le Mariage de Mademoiselle Beulemans*. Both feature the much loved, recently deceased actress Christiane Lenain. A teach-yourself guide to Bruxellois, *Le Bruxellois en 70 Leçons* caused considerable media interest when published in 1999. I had assumed it was a joke. But author Georges Lebouc appears to take the subject remarkably seriously.

Bruxellois native speakers are typified by the old men that you find propping up bars in the Place du Jeu de Balle of a morning. Their turns of phrase have most locals in hysterics, and the population does use certain Bruxellois terms to add humor to a conversation. But as with using Cockney rhyming slang, the comic effect is only as good as your attempt to mimic the accent. Use copious **rkh** sounds where an **r** should do. Stress other consonants that lie dormant in French. And spice up your speech with a few linguistic malapropisms. "*Ça dépend de ce que vous voulez dire*" in correct French, would be "*Ça depende de quoi ske tu veux dire*" in Bruxellois.

Another way to get a Bruxellois twang is to use the suffix *-ke* (effectively a version of the Flemish *tje*, meaning little) to certain French words. For example, in French *une fille* is a girl, *ma fille* is my daughter, while (dangerously) *fille* said alone is prostitute. In Bruxellois, adding the *-ke* suffix to the word takes away the sting; *filleke* is a friendly, jovial way of saying young lady.

Belgian German

Although German is spoken by a tiny minority of Belgians, specialist linguists have still managed to divide Belgian German into two sub-dialects: Ripuarisch, spoken in Eupen and Mosel Franconian, in St Vith. Either tend to somewhat harden the throaty German **ch** sound to a harder **k** and give the **i** sound a more Dutch **ij** twang.

The official German-language community is recognized in nine municipalities of the Ostkantonen (Eastern Cantons) area along the country's eastern border (notably Eupen and St Vith). It has limited legal powers, and autonomy in matters relating to culture, health, and education. Public services are in German and officials must be able to speak the language, although many signs are bilingual (with French). Classes in schools are conducted in the German medium but as there

51

are no universities for the German-speaking population in Belgium, students need to be bilingual in French or Flemish, or must proceed across the border for higher education.

NAMES

People's Names
Many Christian names have different forms in French, Flemish, and English. With people you meet, there's no need to attempt a translation. But with monarchs, historical figures, and especially saints (and thus church names), it can be useful to know each form. While some are very similar (*Nicholas* and *Niklaas*, *Marie* and *Maria*) some are more divergent (See Glossary). Traditionally, many Francophones were christened with three Christian names, of which the last was frequently Ghislain/Ghislaine —a superstitious mantra for good health. Note that Belgian women keep their original family names after marriage, although their children adopt the father's surname.

What's in a Name?
You might think that it's easy enough to guess by someone's surname, which language they speak. In fact it's almost impossible. Francophone families with Dutch sounding names are common, as are Flemish family names with a distinctly French twang. The one thing that is fairly certain is that a *de* in front of the surname indicates someone of "breeding." Such surnames in Belgium carry similar nuances as double-barreled names in modern Britain—classy or snobby according to your perspective. Originally they simply showed where a family came from; *de* literally means of. Hence, the derivation of the unfortunate name *de Ath* whose forbears may be traced back to the Hainaut town of Ath, besieged by Louis XIV in 1667.

*This memorial to a great Brussels mayor is bilingual—he's
Charles Buls in French and Karel Buls in Flemish*

Geopolitical Names

There's plenty to get confused about. Single geographical terms often represent an entity whose extent has varied substantially over time. Flanders once stretched well into what is now France. There's a Limburg Province in the Netherlands as well as one in Belgium. Liège, like Namur and Antwerp, is the name of a city as well as that of a province, and historically was an independent prince-bishopric. Luxembourg (or Luxemburg) might refer to the independent Grand Duchy or to the Belgian province.

Just as many foreigners don't appreciate the difference between *the British Isles* (the U.K. and Ireland), *the United Kingdom* (a nation state) and *Great Britain* (geographical term for the biggest island of the U.K.), so some people get mixed up with the terms *Low Countries* (a geographical term referring to the Netherlands and Belgium), *Netherlands* (a nation state of the EU), and *Holland* (a province of the Netherlands, although often incorrectly used colloquially to refer to the whole of the Netherlands).

Tourist offices have created an additional confusion by marketing the whole of Wallonia under the title *Ardennes*, though the latter is geographically limited to the hilly southeastern corner of the region.

Bilingual Place Names

Outside Brussels, road signs tend to use only the local language version of a name. This is fine for street signs but gets ludicrous for signs pointing to faraway places: e.g. Flemish motorway signs for Paris and Lille in France point you to Parijs and Rijsel respectively. In Wallonia signs directing you to the Hague and Aachen will show "La Haye" and "Aix-la-Chapelle" respectively. And that's nothing compared to the confusion between Belgian town names which can be as varied as Mons = Bergen or Jezus-Eik = Notre-Dame-au-Bois (See Glossary). And by the way, Uitrit is not the name of a town, but the term for *exit*. You'll see this posted along motorways in Flanders, as well as pointing to the route out of towns.

Street signs around the Rue Haute in Brussels are sometimes trilingual in French, Flemish, and Bruxellois.

NONVERBAL COMMUNICATION

Gestures

Although not necessarily unique to Belgium, there are a few interesting gesticulations to watch out for.

(He's/she's) drunk   a loosely clenched fist, twisted swiftly about the nose. Accompanied by a manic grimace

(He's/she's) gay	make a loose fist with your left hand, then gently slap it with your right
Getting nervous!!	Hand held vertically, bring thumb and fingers together, rhythmically simulating a beating heart
You're talking too much	As in the U.K., "rabbiting on" is suggested by flapping the thumb up toward the other four fingers held horizontally simulating a chattering mouth—rather like Rod Hull's "Emu" and is meant to be a sign to shut you up.
F*** off	Raising the right forearm jerkily against the left fist, or the similarly insulting "one finger salute, are as potentially dangerous in Belgium as they are elsewhere. However, these are also used fairly casually as jokes between good friends—so think twice before getting angry.

Kissing

Greeting people is a nightmare. Should you kiss their cheeks? If so should you really go through with the full Belgian quota of three kisses. Which cheek first? I've put this question to a wide number of Belgians and the fact is that nobody seems to have hard and fast rules. Basically do kiss the cheeks of close friends and relations, regardless of sex, and follow them for a lead as to the direction and kiss count.

SYMBOLS

Just as Wales has its dragon and Ireland its shamrock, so Flanders is depicted by a lion and Wallonia by a rooster. The two creatures are frequently caricatured in cartoons, whether fighting or bound together by a restraining single crown. Brussels has its own symbol—a stylized yellow iris on a blue ground which is said to have been the original inspiration for France's *fleur de lys* motif.

Chapter Five

SOCIAL INSTITUTIONS

On both sides of the linguistic divide, Catholicism has been a defining feature of the culture for centuries. Yet despite deep roots, it is seen from an objective angle and remains open to mockery. This is typical of the levelheaded practicality and self-deprecating sense of humor that are such prominent aspects of the national character. There is a similar curious ambivalence to many other social institutions including marriage and the family.

RELIGION

Catholic Majority

The vast majority of the population, whether Francophone or Flemish, consider themselves at least nominally Roman Catholic. You'll notice plenty of little Madonna and saint figures in niches and grottoes if you keep your eyes open.

When the Low Countries were divided after the Dutch Revolt, Holland escaped from Spain's barbed Catholic grip. But despite the initially strong resistance, the inquisition was allowed to get its teeth deep into the Belgian soul. By the end of the 19th century, religious differences with the Dutch had grown too wide to allow a permanent reunion of the Low Countries. This proved a key factor in the very creation of Belgium.

While Catholicism remains deeply rooted, as with all things Belgian, religion is rarely allowed to stand in the way of practicality. Unlike more conservative Catholics in countries like Ireland, few Belgians seem hopelessly mired in guilt or overshadowed by papal dogma. Divorce may not be entirely straightforward, but it's a fact of life. Birth control has long been accepted as normal and sensible. Abortion was legalized in 1990. One devout septuagenarian believer candidly told me that she discounted the Pope as a senile old man, embarrassing to the real faithful and not worth taking seriously.

Nonetheless, religious "tourism" is still an important activity. Pilgrims have been visiting Scherpenheuvel near Diest since the 14th century when a miraculous statuette of the Virgin appeared, stuck to a tree. These days, people converge here the first Sunday of November, but superstitious drivers come year round to have their new cars blessed by a priest. For those without the time or money to go to the real thing, Belgium has its own mini Lourdes at the hamlet of Banneux where the young Mariette Beco reputedly saw eight visions of the Virgin Mary in 1933. The village has since attracted over 400,000 of the faithful who come during the healing season (May–October). Quite coincidentally, many of the shops and souvenir stalls just happen to be run by the Beco family. At Lourdes itself, there are a remarkable number of bars stocked with Belgian beer, ideal for rotund Belgian pilgrims to relax with after a hard day's prayer.

"Looking Catholic"
Belgian friends use the term *Catholic* as a social label. Pointing to a group of people with the comment, "Don't they look Catholic, eh?"

doesn't mean that a gaggle of nuns is waddling past. Instead it means, "Hey, they look classical, well-dressed, and expensively educated (i.e. snobby)". Practically speaking, the Catholic look means pastel colors and pearls for women, Berber jackets for men, and well over 2.2 kids in tow.

Other Christian Groups

In Belgium, the term *Christian* is generally equated unquestioningly with Catholicism unless otherwise indicated. Nonetheless, there are a sprinkling of other denominations, in many cases foreigners and descendants of immigrants. The meetings of several such groups are announced weekly in *The Bulletin.*

Belgians are a tolerant, relatively self-contented people. Few seem to share the insecurities that seem to make cults and "new churches" so popular elsewhere. Mormon missionaries tell me that Belgium is considered a tough posting. Even to a group of people who must be congenitally accustomed to having doors slammed in their faces, Belgians stand out as being unusually disinterested in their brand of salvation.

The Forgotten Muslims

Belgium has a small but growing Muslim minority, which is verging on a majority in one or two inner city communes (e.g. St-Josse in Brussels which in 1995 recorded 39% of its inhabitants to be of Muslim Turkish and North African descent). Although many are second-or third-generation immigrants, they're still considered for-eigners by the majority of society. And in a cultural sense, the Islamic population will always remain foreigners, not just due to a thick streak of xenophobia in the otherwise courteous Belgian soul, but also because good Muslims don't drink alcohol. And how can one be a true Belgian without a beer!

Enlightened first attempts in 1968 to involve immigrant groups in local decision-making brought to the forefront importantly sensitive suggestions such as the setting aside of special areas for Muslim burials in municipal cemeteries. However this idea was not acted upon and only reappeared in the media spotlight in the late 1990s when the body of Loubna Ben Aissa, the Moroccan victim of a pedophile, had to be repatriated to North Africa due to the lack of Islamic burial space in Belgium.

The Jewish Community

The flowing black robes and hair curls of traditionally dressed Hasidic men make Antwerp's modest Jewish community particularly visible, especially around Pelikaanstraat and the diamond district. Yet in reality the less obvious Jewish population of Brussels is around the same size—some 15,000–20,000.

A small group of Ashkenazi Jews who settled in Brabant in the early Middle Ages was largely exterminated by locals who blamed them for poisoning the well water to kill the Christians. This, the locals believed, triggered the onset of the plague in the 14th century. Despite the persecution, the repression of Jews in Spain led to another wave of immigration in the 15th century. Although Spain theoretically controlled the Low Countries at the time, cities like Antwerp initially protected the refugees. Most later continued to non-Catholic Holland where there was less threat of inquisitional attacks, but a small nucleus of less than 40 families lived on in Antwerp against the odds.

Conditions improved after the French Revolution and Belgian independence. Shortly after 1831, the state recognized the Consistoire Central Israélite de Belgique (which brings together Orthodox and secular Jewish organizations) as the official representative body for the Belgian Jewry. The Jewish community grew rapidly, the diamond industry finding jobs for thousands of refugees from the 1880s pogroms in Central Europe. Numbers rose even faster in the years immediately before World War II. In 1940, Belgium itself was invaded by the Nazis, and while many fled further afield, roughly half the Jewish population perished. More information is available at http://amyisrael.co.il/europe/belgium/index.htm and http://www.trabel.com/antwerp/Jewishantwerp.htm.

SUPERSTITIONS

Belgians share many of the superstitions of Western Europe. Bad luck can be brought upon oneself by walking under ladders, breaking a mirror, opening umbrellas indoors, and black cats crossing one's path while driving. If you happen to have a dead relative in the house, don't invite people to pay their last respects on a Sunday.

Like most Westerners, Belgians traditionally consider horseshoes lucky symbols, and will touch wood, cross fingers, or perhaps throw salt over their shoulders to prevent good fortune from souring. Some Belgians think a surefire way to win the lottery (or at least to ensure a healthy income) is to cook pancakes on Shrove Tuesday while holding a coin in one's hand. The numbers 7 and 13 can be lucky or unlucky according to the context. Some of the curious facial hair on show in Marollian cafés may be related to the old superstition that sideburns are a magnet for good fortune, although nowadays the idea has been largely forgotten.

FAMILY

In general, Belgians do not come from tightly knit families. But family ties are extremely strong, nonetheless. As with all Belgian attitudes, the genuine love and care family members shower on one another is tempered with a very sensible dose of practicality. My wife, for example, spent years of her life fussing over her grandmother to keep her happy, healthy, and independent. But she'd have no qualms about popping her into a nursing home if she needed to.

Common to many countries with a Christian background, most children have a godmother, or a *marraine/meter* (French/Flemish) and a godfather, or a *Parrain/Peter* (French/Flemish) whose role is theoretically to ensure that the child has a good Catholic upbringing and respects an acceptable moral code. These days, however, the godparents' main task is to provide a few presents and to be a free babysitter on call. Anyone could, in principle, be a godparent, but the diplomatic Belgian norm is to choose one grandparent from either side of the family.

MARRIAGE

Until recently, marriage was relatively unpopular. This is not just an echo of a pan-Occidental latter-day trend, but also a reaction to the odd fiscal quirk that a married couple was taxed less favorably than

as two individuals, at least until retirement. In Belgium when it comes to a tussle between religion and the national sport of tax evasion, it is fiscal fighting which sounds more appealing. Tax reforms proposed in early October 2000, however, aim to remove the tax disincentive for marriage by treating each partner as an individual for certain calculations, and equalizing tax exempt values between married and single people. Eventually!

Inheritance tax continues for now to favor spouses and direct linear relations (parents-children-grandchildren) at 3–27% compared to 10–50% for cohabitants (35–65% for siblings and 45–65% for non-relations).

When people do tie the knot, betrothal is a quasi-legal contract and traditionally, marriage should follow within six weeks of the official engagement announcement. In reality, it's only the royals who are bound to this conventional time scale. On the wedding day, the first stop for the couple and their witnesses is an office at the commune's town hall. It is there that the legally important civil procedures are conducted, even for those who choose to continue to church for a traditional ceremony.

DIVORCE

Divorce is a minefield of regulations and traps, some of which appear to be very differently interpreted by the different tribunals who oversee such breakups. Divorce by mutual consent is possible after 18 months of marriage but requires both partners to make several personal appearances before these tribunals over a period of several months. If either partner misses a session, the whole procedure returns to square one.

The concept of one partner being at fault is very much alive when it comes to adjudicating divorces. To prove "fault" in cases of adultery requires solid police evidence which can be hard to gather. If a couple has been legally separated for five years, one partner may use the length of separation as grounds for divorce. But in this case, the initiator of the proceedings is considered to be "at fault" and thus may in the future become responsible for alimony payments.

DEATH AND FUNERALS

In Belgium, the assumption is that you want to donate your precious organs to medicine unless you specifically chose otherwise (and make that clear in a declaration lodged at the commune). If you want to have your remains buried in a cemetery, there's an important choice of type. Short-term free plots in the commune's cemetery are recycled twice a decade, so if you don't want to have your memorial stone evicted after five years it's necessary to be interred in a concession, which is a special longer term site where, upon the payment of a suitable rent, the site can be maintained for up to 50 years. There are also rules for the disposal of the ashes of those cremated. Under Belgian law, you are not allowed to sprinkle your ashes at sea—if you desire a maritime end, your *cendres* may be disposed of in a special soluble urn. All funeral and cremation arrangements are handled through Pompes Funèbres/Begrafenisondeming funeral homes.

PETS

Belgians don't quite share the same protective mania Brits have for animals. Although relatively few go on about animal rights—and almost no one has the slightest qualms about wearing fur—Belgians adore their pets. In family restaurants, you can often find a playful puppy. In the streets, you're not likely to be worried by strays, but Belgian dog owners are infamously casual about educating their darlings on the topic of doggy defecation. As a result, city pavements are notoriously full of *crottes/hondenpoep.*

THE BELGIAN HOME

Belgians love their homes and many feel a real need to keep up with the Smets. Hedges should be clipped and lawns regularly mowed, but never, of course, on a Sunday. That's not a religious prohibition but one of noise reduction for those who wish to snooze in their own gardens. Or, perhaps, listen in on their neighbors' conversations.

Where They Live

Far fewer people buy property in Belgium than in the U.K. The reason is not because property prices are high. Indeed, by EU standards they are pretty reasonable. However, by the time you've added up fees, charges, and taxes, you'll have to pay some 20–25% above the actual selling price. Even a hefty rise in house prices would be unlikely to offset those taxes. Thus house-owners wouldn't consider speculative buying and selling to work their way up the property ladder. So once you do buy, it's generally for life. The positive side of this is social stability and a less volatile property market. The negative side is inflexibility and a lot of commuting.

The majority of Belgians rent an apartment or house, typically on renewable three-, six-, or nine-year contracts that leave tenants feeling secure enough to decorate and furnish from scratch. Certain towns such as Leuven have big student populations, but on the whole, school-leavers seek further education in universities close to their parental homes and commute. Thus, there is relatively little in the way of student accommodation.

Building Their Own

U.S.-style condominiums or British-style luxury housing estates are relatively rare in Belgium. There's a "brick in every Belgian belly" according to a popular local saying and almost every Belgian seems to dream of having his/her own home built to order rather than buying someone else's. Yet those who live out this dream seem to fall very far short of the inventiveness of Victor Horta or Paul Hankar, Belgium's great Art Nouveau architects. These days, home designs are usually remarkably staid and stolid and rarely seem to justify all the effort. Whitewashed brick homes in pseudo-farmhouse-style are particularly popular in the suburbs, with heavy wooden shutters and a flower-box or two. Leave the bricks un-whitened if you like the idea of your neighbors passing by with a quiet tut.

After 1995, there was a brief boom in self-building thanks to a new tax relief law that brought value-added tax (VAT) on materials for self-built homes down from 21% to 12%. However, the supply of available land with planning permission was limited, leading to soaring land prices and a rapid return to the status quo. Now, there are even better tax breaks available for the renovation of old houses.

A tradition amongst house builders is to put a branch or a potted plant at the apex of the roofing beams once the frame is completed. This symbolizes the new life arriving with the building's construction. If you want to do this in mid-winter when real saplings are leafless, you can buy an artificial version from DIY shops to keep up appearances.

Home Décor

Naturally everyone has their own way to decorate a house. Unlike neighboring Holland where you can look straight into almost anyone's front room, Belgian houses often maintain their privacy with net curtains. Stereotypically nosy neighbors lurk behind them, rustling amongst the leaves of ornamental sanseveria plants trying to watch unseen what's going on on the street below. Mrs Bucket from the U.K. TV series *Keeping up Appearances* would feel right at home.

Young people with newer homes are less likely to endure or encourage the gloomy, shuttered interiors that seem to be popular with the older generation. Older homes are likely to have religious symbols (a crucifix or a Madonna statuette) tucked away in bedrooms, a penchant the younger generation consider spooky. Lurking in more than a few households are obsessive kitsch-collectors and garden gnome aficionados. TV channels delight in seeking out such citizens and allowing them to show off their prize possessions, much to the embarrassment of their friends and relations.

The Postbox

Outside the city centers, few Belgians receive mail through a slot in the door. Instead, like American suburban homes, the norm is a separate postbox at the end of the drive or front garden. The three most typical, no-nonsense designs are the simple bread-bin style boxes,

Like garden gnomes, postboxes allow suburban Belgian families to exhibit individuality, taste, and refinement.

hollow brick gateposts, or metal pentagons. However, more than a few Belgians have decided that postboxes represent important fashion statements. The much copied trend in nouveau riche suburbs is to buy super-heavy monoliths in filigree cast iron somewhat reminiscent of half-sized Victorian Royal Mail boxes. Occasionally these are even painted red and sometimes confuse passing British tourists into depositing a letter or two. The design has the further advantage of being unmistakably expensive in as understated a way as could be. However, they are also a tempting target for any thieves with suitable lifting equipment.

House-owners wishing to convey a more trendy, youthful image invest in shiny aluminium tubelike postboxes. Americans will be bemused to know that what is fundamentally the standard mailbox in the United States is a fashion item here.

Things get worse. Belgian postmen have to drop letters into mini-windmills, gnome mushrooms, animal mouths, carriages, barrels, nymphs, and little model houses. For those with a love of kitsch, a survey of the postboxes along the suburban roads and avenues can enliven even the dullest day in an unpromising town.

LAW AND ORDER

The law is there to be broken. Rules are not taken as morally important and if a Belgian can get away with something, he/she will try. This would probably be the same in most countries, but in Belgium the fact is that people *can* get away with things. Tax avoidance is the "national sport" and there's an almost total disregard for most traffic rules. Curiously, however, people are very careful where they park their cars. Traffic wardens *do* patrol with the steady ruthlessness of urban tigers. And those little towaway symbols outside garage doors are not just for decoration.

To get an idea of the otherwise liberal attitude of the traffic police, listen to the daily radio announcements which list where speed traps will be placed that day. A traffic policeman interviewed in a local magazine was quoted as saying, "We have to make sure traffic runs smoothly. If someone does something seriously illegal, then we write down the license plate. But otherwise we're not very strict."

That's fine. But serious crime is also rising. Arsonists regularly take on the insurance industry in blatant fashion. Security van drivers delivering cash to banks got so fed up with being robbed en route that they went on strike. TV news shows chuckle at occasional outrageous criminal attempts to rip cash machines from the walls of banks and shops using tow trucks, excavators, and winches. But burglary is becoming so common that people are feeling palpably more insecure. And the biggest perceived danger is car-jacking (theft of your vehicle at gun point at a red light or outside your home in your own garage!). Don't put up a fight and you shouldn't get hurt. The most popular targets are generally company vehicles. On average, 104 cars per day get stolen and even members of parliament have been victims of car-jacking—one minister twice! It all sounds pretty bad, but may boil down to the fact that in a small country, more of the crimes reach the news. In a bigger country like the U.K., national news is less likely to cover every burnt warehouse.

Despite the lackluster policing, Belgium is pretty safe. In 1999, the number of crimes committed in Brussels came to a total of 98,259 reported cases, of which only approximately 11% were violent. There's little reason to fear the streets of Brussels even as you stumble home drunk at 5 a.m.

HERITAGE

A term "Brusselization" has been coined to mean the turning of a beautiful, historic city into one of bland mediocrity through poorly considered renovation and rebuilding. Actually, despite the huge scars of the EU district and other ill-conceived "improvements" Brussels is still remarkably attractive and has around 80 sites and 270 monuments under protection. But that number is relatively low compared with other European capitals. Compared to the U.K. where almost any demolition requires years of enquiry, the rules by which the worth of old buildings are assessed seem relatively lax in Belgium. The public is generally cynical, believing that big money will inevitably sideline public consultations, so rarely puts up much of a fight when historic buildings are threatened.

However, this doesn't mean that the Belgian people aren't proud or interested in their heritage. Far from it. Heritage Days in Brussels, Wallonia, and Flanders open the doors to hundreds of interesting sites every year according to an annual theme. On such days, access is granted to public buildings that are normally closed to the general public. These might include dramatic Art Nouveau commune halls, austere national and European parliament buildings, or demure 1950s school halls. The 1999 Brussels Heritage Days brought around 150,000 visitors to the city. The city took the opportunity to declare protected the grandiose 19th century Palais de Justice—the biggest 19th century building in all Europe. The general public reaction was one of horrified disbelief. Although unpopular when it was built (its builder Joseph Poelaert was disdainfully dubbed the *skieven architekt* or the twisted architect) it is now a great landmark. Everyone had assumed that it had been protected for years. If the Palais de Justice wasn't on the list, what is?

Belgians love their forests and the mildly attractive landscapes which survive in some corners of the country. These spots of nature are a favorite with dog-walking weekenders, joggers, and cyclists. But this love rarely translates into a mass movement to protect threatened areas; as they have with their cities, pragmatic Belgians quickly accept the inevitability of destruction that is a by-product of further development.

Chapter Six

THE BELGIAN PEOPLE

Think of Belgium (Flanders and Wallonia) as a traditional, married couple who have long ago realized they're incompatible. They do the dishes together without talking, but keep up public appearances for the sake of the children.

Just below the surface Belgium appears to be an unstable, heterogeneous society (See Chapter Four). But contrary to popular belief, there is a deeper sense of Belgian-ness which transcends the antagonistic linguistic divisions, regional individualities, and social strata. This is manifested in the self-deprecating sense of humor, the practicality, and ability to compromise. Mutual distrust between the linguistic groups is real enough, but is not as strong as the shared Belgian disdain of foreigners. And despite an apparent lack of patriotism, there is a great, understated national pride in the success of famous Belgians and all things Belgian.

BASIC SOCIAL DIVISIONS

Belgium's social divisions are drawn along the lines of language (predominantly Flemish or French) and of socio-political class: Catholic (conservative, snobby, and rich), Liberal (also well off, and also Catholic, but more discreet about it!), and Socialist (poorer or more radical). This applies to political parties (as explained in Chapter Four), but also to trade unions and even in education. In addition there are strong regional identities that may not be immediately obvious to the outsider. People are proud to be linguistically Flemish or Francophone. Yet very few would ever cite Flanders or Wallonia as home. If asked where he/she comes from, a proud Fleming would more likely say, "Antwerp" or "Gent" and not "Flanders." It's fun to be aware of the stereotypes associated with each town or district, though naturally these are potentially dangerous over-generalizations.

Aalst	unrefined, ugly accent
Antwerp	permissive; "going to Antwerp?" said with a wink between men, might suggest a night of seedy debauchery. Also famed for a superiority complex. "Going to *stad*" (Going to town) refers to Antwerp as though no other town existed.
Bruges	civilized, conservatively Catholic, staid
Charleroi	poor, industrial, full of Italians, cheerful but short-tempered

Gent	raunchy and radical (compared to Bruges). Stubborn and independent minded "noose-wearers" (*stroppen-dragers*).
Hasselt	snobby, superior (but for no obvious reason)
Kortrijk	traditional, strongly Catholic, snobby show-offs (but genuinely wealthy)
Leuven	radical and staunchly Flemish
Limburg	ponderous, slow
Mechelen	rich, narrow-minded "moon extinguishers" (from fable "Maneblussers" in which the townsfolk were tricked into believing that their town hall was on fire—it was simply illuminated by reflected moonlight).
Mons	traditional, staid
Namur	backward, boring
Ostend	worldly wise, persuasive

SELF-IMAGE

How does a Belgian sum up his/her own national characteristics? "Ah ...we're the country of great individualism," claimed one local journalist, "We have Magritte, Tintin, Jacques Brel…" Sadly of late, he admits, the image has been somewhat tainted by some pretty unpleasant brushes with crime, food contamination, and pedophilia. So is Belgium really a nest of evil, rotten to the core? For the neighboring Dutch, that is just what they have always imagined of Belgium. But the Belgian answer is that everybody's got the same troubles; Belgians are just more open about their failures. "It's a national masochism," explained the journalist over half a dozen beers. But it hurts deeply those who try to maintain the façade of the little rainy paradise.

NATIONALISM

Pure Belgian nationalists are about as common as Martini-sipping mullahs in Mecca. But this doesn't preclude a strong national pride. My Belgian wife loves Belgium. She thinks it's one of the best countries in the world. She likes the compact convenience, the standard of living, the social system, the health service, and the ease of going anywhere else from here. These are archetypal Belgian choices, calm, logical, and based on rational benefits. When it comes to more traditional measures of nationalism, she falls flat. Once, I asked her to sing the national anthem. Standing to attention, chin in the air she started as though singing for a packed stadium:

"Oh cherished Belgium, sainted land of our fathers

Our soul and our hearts are…are….are…"

The stiff pose vanished and she collapsed, laughing, "I don't even know the words!" Worse, she has twice humiliated herself by mixing up the Belgian and German flags, saying, "Well they look much alike, don't they?"

Belgium and the EU

So, Belgium's good because life is straightforward and convenient here. Not because it's Belgium per se. That explains the Belgians' very positive attitude to European integration. While Britain is afraid of losing something indefinable yet distinctively British, the Belgians see it purely as added convenience and practicality and thus offering an improvement in living standards.

The Euro? "Great idea. No more exchange problems when we drive to France to buy wine," they say. Even the older generation appears to have no significant qualms over swapping the Belgian franc for a pan-European currency. And in a state that's already heavily regionalized, the possibility of an eventual "United States of Europe" is no spectre, as it seems to be for Britain. Just a logical idea. And a lucrative one for Belgium—with Brussels as its capital.

IMAGES OF OTHER COUNTRIES

The following is a list of stereotypical ideas Belgians have of certain other countries and their people:

Country	Negative	Positive
U.K.	high cost of living, terrible health service	lower property taxes atmospheric country pubs
U.S.	tax and tips extra plastic smiles	24-hour supermarkets efficient service cheap petrol
Dutch	tight-fisted	liberal broad-minded, clean
French	uptight, temperamental	cheap wine lovely country
Germany	dull, conformist	hardworking straightforward

VIEW OF FOREIGNERS

Immigrants in Belgium are viewed with the curious ambivalence common to many European nations. The attitude to the relatively small community of Congolese is slightly patronizing but generally positive; they are usually thought of as law-abiding, generally well-educated, honorary Belgians. Italians in the Charleroi area are virtually invisible and are increasingly well-integrated into society. In fact, they are no longer considered foreigners.

Turks and North Africans are treated with vastly less tolerance. Many Belgians see these groups as social security swindlers sending money to extended families abroad. The North Africans in particular are held responsible for most of the country's petty crime. On the positive side, Turkish, Greek, and North African shops and restaurants are popular because they are cheaper, more creative, and open longer hours than many Belgian equivalents. Especially in Francophone Belgium, Turkish and North African shopkeepers are considered unusually friendly, in part because they insist on the using the familiar forms of the French language (See Chapter Four). This is a curious paradox because such cutesy parlance would be thought cheeky or downright impudent coming from a local.

Attitudes to Tourism

If you've been in bustling Bruges vainly looking for a hotel room, you might remember Belgium with less than glowing warmth. And if you've peeped into the tacky Brussels souvenir shops decked with inferior lace, you might be tempted to think that the Belgian tourist industry is coldheartedly commercial.

Bruges sees so many millions of weekenders from every corner of Northern Europe that it's hardly surprising that service occasionally slips. But the reality almost everywhere else is that tourism seems curiously uncommercial. Almost every little town and village has a tourist office producing sheaves of listings, historical information, walking ideas, beautiful maps, and colorful brochures. Yet one suspects many do so because that's what they're meant to do. These same offices often seem surprised and intrigued to find that anyone actually comes. "You're a tourist? In Belgium? Why?" It's as though they share a sense of disbelief that anyone would, of their own volition, prefer to visit Belgium over France or Holland. "Amsterdam is so much more beautiful," said one very self-deprecating Antwerp resident.

BELGIAN HUMOR

Belgians don't like to take Belgium too seriously. And those Belgians who do so are suitably vilified. The Flemish David Letterman, Rob Vanoudenhoven, cheekily kicked off a TV interview with the chief minister of Flanders, saying, "So you're 'Minister President' of the region—that sounds a bit pompous and pretentious doesn't it?" One of his XII Werken van Vanoudenhoven shows launched an "I love Wallonia" campaign amusingly seeking out Walloon mediocrity. Meanwhile, a regular Sunday night pseudo-documentary *À la Flamande* gently pokes fun at Flemish eccentrics by giving them the chance to demonstrate a gamut of weird hobbies to a TV camera.

Belgian Stories

"Oh that's a Belgian story," my wife declares every time we hear a new, nonsensical news story that, she claims, could never happen elsewhere. Take two stories on a typical day in October 1999.

Headline news was of a twelve-year-old boy who had broken into the Brussels tram museum and driven off in one of their street cars. An interview with a tram driver revealed a certain respect for the child who must have researched rather carefully to have been able to operate the vehicle. Oh, and by the way, the parents will be billed for all the disruption caused.

Later in the day was a stranger story still. In the village of Frameries, an audacious gang of thieves had stolen the roof from the local school. "Yes," said the bemused headmaster, "I too assumed it was a joke when somebody called me." But sure enough, a gang had, with unimaginable daring, removed all the galvanized strips from the roof. Despite making all kinds of noise, nobody had raised an alarm and they'd made off with some thousands of francs worth of scrap metal. The reporter summed up deliciously that the school's staff had not planned to extend their open-door policy to an open-roof one.

Jokes

The most obvious form of Belgian joke pokes fun at the "other" linguistic community like Polak jokes in the US, Irish jokes in the UK, or Kerryman jokes in Ireland. Take the following conversation…

"I've got a good joke about the Walloons,"

"Watch it, I am Walloon!"

"Don't worry, I can tell it three times!"

(If told by a Francophone simply replace the word *Walloon* with *Flemish*.)

But it's not just Flemish–Walloon differences that are the butt of mutual ribbing. There are similar regional jokes based on local stereotypes. Thus a Fleming from Gent might make the following dig at someone from Limburg:

"Name one Third World colony in Belgium".

Answer: "Limbabwe!"

Similarly Namurites are thought of as slow amongst Belgian Francophones. A much repeated joke relates three old men sitting on a roadside bench in Namur. A red sports cars squeals past. For five minutes nobody moves, then one says, "Hey. Nice Ferrari." Ten minutes later it goes by again. After a long silence, the second man says, "But it's a Porsche!" Eventually, the car passes once more and a few minutes later the third man gets to his feet. Grumpily he mutters, "If you two don't stop arguing, I'm going home!"

Belgian jokes don't have to be sectarian. The following is a national classic:

A Belgian driver approaches a low bridge in a four-meter truck.

"Watch out," says his mate, "the sign says 'max height three meters'."

"No problem," says the driver. "There aren't any cops."

Either linguistic group recognizes themselves in this gag where the character's stupidity is egged on by that age-old Belgian passion: beating the law.

The other great element of Belgian humor is the ironic "laugh or else you'll cry" observation. A common butt is the Carrefour Leonard

(See Chapter Eight), an infamous intersection on the Brussels Ring where tailbacks, traffic jams, and appalling accidents have become a daily matter of course. Rather than complain, Belgians wheel out the black humor:

"This week it seems that the world's population has reached six billion. But science remains incapable of explaining why they all meet at the Carrefour Leonard every morning."

Similarly self-mocking was Jean-Claude Defossé's classic *Travaux Inutiles* TV show and "guidebook." Literally translated as Useless Constructions, it was a hard-hitting yet humorous catalogue of Belgium's shockingly large collection of apparently pointless public works: bridges with no access roads, buildings built but never furnished, etc.

Going Too Far?

While they're very happy to joke at their own expense and about other areas of the country, Belgians' tendency to extend such jokes to racial minorities can often appear overtly racist. Belgium was given the dubious privilege of being rated the EU's most racist country following a report by the European Monitoring Centre on Racism and Xenophobia. One in four Belgians polled admitted with unguarded candor that they were "intolerant" toward minority groups.

As it is in many countries, humor is often a political tool in Belgium. The classic example is Noël Godin, who is widely known as the *entarteur* or pie thrower. It is his self-proclaimed mission to splat the faces of any celebrity he considers pretentious, narcissistic, or snobbish. And do it again later if they don't have the sense of humor to laugh it off. Microsoft's Bill Gates was one of his many victims. While few of his fellow Belgians would go as far, Godin's actions bring a great sense of moral justice, a victory for the little person against authority, plus a funny spectacle.

GOSSIP

Belgians love to gossip. Despite being publicly proud that their country doesn't have a tabloid press, many will voraciously flick through the pages of *Gala*, *People*, or *Paris Match* for the latest dirt on anyone in the limelight. The Monica Lewinsky affair was lapped up with glee. But Belgian gossip is fueled by interest rather than a tendency to judge. So when King Albert was found to have fathered a child with another woman, the affair neither evoked horror nor brought down the monarchy. The issue died down within a week or so.

WOMEN'S ISSUES

In practical ways, Belgium is outwardly egalitarian across the genders. Married women have never been expected to change their surnames (although children take the father's surname). At work, there's legal provision for prenatal and maternity leave, laws against sexual harassment, etc. However, there are still plenty of working wives willing (and expected) to come home and cook the potatoes for their beer-swilling men. Women have only had the right to vote since 1948. Although female politicians are well represented, only four out of the 18 cabinet ministers are women. Generally, Belgians are tolerant of what might be termed sexism elsewhere. "I bet that's a women driving," my wife would say about a badly driven car.

Miss Belgique/Miss Belgie/Miss Belgium

The first recorded beauty contest was held in Spa in August 1888. This tradition perhaps explains why one of the country's biggest annual televisual events is Miss Belgium. Even if you find such shows nauseating, they're interesting for the display of national unity—all candidates are expected to chat in both French and Flemish. And so are the guest stars. For the 2000 show, singer Sandra Kim switched from French to Flemish to English in her rendition of the theme song.

ATTITUDES TO MEDICINE

There's an undoubted hypochondriac streak in the national character. Rustle around in most Belgian homes and you'll find a cupboard comprehensively stashed with pills and medicaments. When queried, the Belgian would say, "I don't like taking pills but, hey, why suffer?" This attitude is reflected in the apparent profitability of the pharmacy trade. Some even offer loyalty bonuses of up to 10%. Not bad for people on 100% insurance schemes who, having claimed back their medicine fees, can then get this bonus as cash in pocket.

Normally a pretty modest bunch, the Belgians are rather proud of their healthcare system. And justifiably so since it is one of the best in the world—cheaper than in the United States and much quicker and more flexible than in the U.K. Recent laughs at the expense of the British medical system included a cartoon showing a patient in an English hospital receiving a transfusion of dogs' urine. The caption reads: "Whoops, sorry. At least it's free."

SEX AND PROSTITUTION

Visitors over the centuries have remarked on the sanguine savvy of Belgian women. Sir William Temple found local girls in the 17th century quite ready to use sex to their advantage but noted that their passions "seem to run lower and cooler here than in other contreys where I have converst". The Spanish entourage of Philip II visiting in 1549 came to similar conclusions that women here were "naturally cold" and free from the lusty passions that confound girls in more Mediterranean climes.

Lusty or otherwise, Belgium is certainly not a prudish place. Catholic or not, it takes its liberal lead from the Netherlands. I was astounded to find that established companies took their employees and business guests to places like Brussels' Chez Flo—a rather raunchy transvestite cabaret. But why not! The oldest profession is very visible around Brussels' North Station, with plenty of the red-light flesh windows more typically associated with Amsterdam. And locally, Antwerp has a sin city image, appropriate for Europe's second biggest port. Even in rural areas you'll notice windowless nightclubs dotted along the three lane "national roads". The names of the nightclubs, like Pussy Galore or Love Shack, are as unsubtle as their drinks are exorbitant.

TV news announced, without a snigger, the creation of a school for prostitutes as part of a scheme aimed at improving working conditions. There are limits, however. Payoke, Antwerp's center for prostitutes, had to fire its coordinator in 1999 when it was revealed that proposed "training courses" practised at least five acts that would be considered criminal offences.

When the police do crack down on prostitution, it is generally to liberate captive foreign women. True to the Belgian sense of humor, a sweep of Brussels brothels in 1999 was code-named "Operation Moore" after Demi Moore, star of the film *Striptease*.

HOMOSEXUALITY

Attitudes to homosexuality are not harsh. Homosexuals have been quietly accepted as a part of society. One government minister, suspected of having been a pedophile, later revealed that his gay partner was not a minor. The relief at the revelation that he was "only" a normal gay, proved to be a boost to his popularity. Even in the Church, the gay priest Rudy Borremans continued to serve his flock despite several reprimands for breaking the vow of celibacy. He was finally suspended when he was deemed to have pushed things too far with a book on the difficulties of being homosexual in the Church.

Many cities have an official gay meeting place and associations, and since 2000, Belgium has officially recognized unions between couples of the same sex, or so called "gay marriages," through the Statutory Cohabitation Contract.

ROBBING THE CRADLE

In between running Congo as a personal allotment and glorifying Brussels with grandiose imperial buildings, King Leopold II had an insatiable libido to fuel. At the turn of the century, though approaching 70 years old, he was spending much of his time with a teenage prostitute by the name of Caroline Lacroix, who would later be the mother of two of his illegitimate royal children. Leopold had also been named amongst the clients of a London madam, Mrs Jeffries, who was indicted for procuring prepubescent sex slaves. He never denied it.

Now, a century after Leopold, the bad name he brought upon his country remains. During the mid-1990s when I first came to live here, you'd see hundreds of little fliers on which were printed the innocent faces of missing children. Unlike the ever changing mugshots on American milk cartons these Belgian faces were always the same few. The case involving Marc Dutroux, who had long been suspected of supplying children to a pedophile ring before he was arrested, exposed the slack attitude of the police and their blundering. Apparently, when the police visited Dutroux's house months before he finally surrendered, they simply asked if there was a secret chamber with some kids in it. "No," said Dutroux, and the cops and went away. Dutroux finally admitted to kidnapping and murdering some of the missing children. But one of the girls, Loubna Ben Aissa, remained long unaccounted for. She was found dead, eventually, killed by an altogether different sex offender. People really started to doubt their own society. There came the era of the White Marches against the state and the apathetic police. For much of 1997, people took to the streets every weekend to demand answers. In the wake of the White Marches, Belgium has developed a well-publicized Child Focus hotline which very rapidly mobilizes search squads and coordinates poster campaigns if children are reported missing. Dial 110.

NATURISM

At travel fairs, I am often surprised to see the many stands related to naturism. Yes, naturism as in public nudity. My wife, however, was more surprised at my reaction. "We're not prudes," she reminded me and named a couple of friends and cousins who, as it transpired, were themselves naturists.

If you like the idea of throwing off all your clothes with a group of equally unself-conscious people, you'll be pleased to know that a Belgian nudist beach finally opened in Bredene in summer 2001, and that there are in fact no less than 17 naturist associations in Belgium. Most have swimming pools, saunas, and gym facilities and some organize open-air sporting activities, although perhaps not during the winter. For more information contact FBN and The International Naturist Federation which is based in Antwerp.

FAMOUS BELGIANS

"Bet you can't name five famous Belgians," taunt friends who hear that I'm living in Euroland. Ironically, the two Belgians that spring most rapidly to many minds aren't even real: Tintin, the quiffed cartoon boy and Hercule Poirot, Agatha Christie's hallmark detective, who was constantly grumbling that people think he's French.

However, you may find that you know more Belgians than you realize. The following are some notable examples: the great artists Anthony van Dyck, Peter Paul Rubens, Pieter Breughel and the "Flemish primitives" who invented oil painting. James Ensor, and surrealist Rene Magritte took Belgian art into the 20th century along with cartoonists like Hergé and great Art Nouveau architect Victor Horta. Musicians from Django Reinhardt to Plastic Bertrand to dEUS are/were all Belgian, as was the greatest ever "French" singer Jacques Brel. Eddy Merckx (arguably the most famous cyclist ever) and Jacky Ickx (the motor sports champion) plastered Belgian "ckx"s on to the sporting record books. Jean-Claude Van Damme is known to many as the "Muscles from Brussels." Fewer people know that Audrey Hepburn was also born there.

It's worth familiarizing yourself with some of the famous and the lesser-known Belgian stars. Such knowledge is a really useful tool for fitting in and showing locals that you're interested in their culture. A small selection of names is given below, with many more in the arts and sports sections of Chapter Twelve.

Leaders and Religious Figures

OK, so Belgium doesn't jump to mind for flamboyant high profile leaders. The infamous, bushy-bearded Leopold II was probably the most memorable if not best loved Belgian king. But Charles V, the greatest Hapsburg Holy Roman Emperor was born in Gent (See Chapter Two) and several other historically significant leaders were born in what is now Belgium.

Few Brits realize that their English-Norman kings were so full of Belgian blood. In fact, William the Conqueror's mother Arletta was from Florennes (south of Charleroi) and his wife Mathilde was daughter of the count of Flanders (Baldwin V). The English crown might have had another strong dose of Belgian blood in the 16th century had the fake "Richard IV" of England come to power. In 1495, a Walloon named Perkin Warbeck working as a merchant's servant in Ireland was "discovered" to be one of the sons of England's Edward IV. In reality those sons had actually been killed in the Tower of London; but whether blind, bribed, or just potty, Margaret, Duchess of Burgundy, seemed to recognize Perkin as her nephew Richard. Eventually, with the help of scheming Scotland, Perkin attempted to invade England to claim his "rightful throne" from Henry VII. He managed to take Cornwall while his Scots allies skirmished in Northumberland, but in the end, the pretender was sent to the Tower of London just like the boy he'd imitated. The whole escapade was probably funded by Maximillian the Austro-Belgian Holy Roman Emperor.

Impress your friends by revealing that Clovis I (465–511), the first major figure of the French Merovingian dynasty was born in Tournai. He created the first Frankish kingdom to cover all of Gaul (France), and his empire provided the eventual launching pad for "King of Hearts" Charlemagne albeit with plenty of complexities in the interim. If you want to be a real smart arse, you could go on to mention that the first European "king" of Jerusalem was Godfrey de Bouillon, (1066–1099) the Belgian baron who bankrolled much of the dubious first Crusade by mortgaging his Ardennes estates. Actually he was "too modest" to use the title "king" (preferring "Guardian of the Holy Sepulcre") but not shy to lead the massacre of some 40,000 Muslims and Jews—that's what a pious man did in the eleventh century after all. His brother Baldwin I (Baudouin I) kept Jerusalem "Belgian" until 1118. And another Baudouin (Baldwin X of Flanders) was later to become the first crusader king of Byzantium (Istanbul). For the ultimate in Belgian trivia, reveal that Pope Adrian VI (1459–1523) was Flemish, born Adrian Florensz and previously a teacher at the then fairly new Leuven University where he educated the young Charles V in 1507. Or that the movie *Molokai* was based on the life of Belgian missionary Father Damien (1840–1889) who devoted his life to helping lepers in the Hawaiian Islands, eventually dying of the disease there.

Scientists and Inventors

If you've always thought that Greenland is about the size of Africa, it's a Fleming named Gerhard Kremer (1512–1594) that you have to blame. Better known as Gerardus Mercator, his Mercator cylindrical projection still remains more popular than the equal area Peters projection, which makes the world look inelegantly stretched. Optimistically touted as Belgium's Leonardo Da Vinci, Simon Stevin (1548–1620) was the mathematician, physicist, and great medieval all-rounder credited with devising the decimal system. Over three centuries later, it was Belgian astronomer Georges Lemaître who proposed the idea of an "evolving universe" though he remains overshadowed by his more famous friend Einstein. At least five Belgians have won Nobel prizes for medicine or science during the 20th century.

If you visit the attractive town of Dinant, you'll find a rather odd looking topiary bush in the shape of a saxophone. It commemorates the locally born inventor of that instrument, Adolph Sax (1814–1894). U.S. President Clinton popped by to play a tune in his honor.

Chapter Seven

SETTLING IN

TRIGG.

The strain of moving to a new place is always pretty intense. Even though many Belgians do speak great English, the language as well as the cultural barriers don't help make things any easier. The first thing you'll need is a good impartial source of advice.

Fortunately there's plenty of help to be had. The wonderful Community Help Service offers advice in English to anyone who needs it. They have an office at rue St Georges 102, Box 20, 1050 Brussels, tel 02 647 6780 and operate a 24-hour information and crisis line (02 648 4014) where you can seek help with any problem. There's also the weekly English-language weekly *The Bulletin* which lists meetings of expatriate societies and associations. It also produces the extremely helpful *Newcomer* supplement twice a year (free for subscribers). The latter has all the latest details on housing, paperwork, schools, etc. There is also a very helpful website aimed directly at English-speaking expatriates in Belgium at http://www.xpats.com.

RESIDENCY DOCUMENTS

To get a residence permit or identification card you need to locate the *maison communale/gemeentehuis* of the commune you are residing in to register as a commune resident. You have to do this within eight days of arrival. Take along your passport and some photos and money to pay the local tax. You may also be asked for a copy of your lease or accommodation arrangements. Ironically the latter may require you to have an identity card to start with! Non-EU citizens will need a residence visa and a work permit. The visa must be applied for before arrival and the employer in Belgium needs to append the work permit to a copy of the employment contract. The employer must also confirm that there is no local labor to fill the post.

Once you have registered with the commune, you should receive a temporary residence permit which will allow you to stay for three months. You can extend your stay to five years if you can prove that you have filed an application for self-employment registration or that you've got a job. Evidence of previous social security payments is also expected and you may need a medical certificate, passport, photos, and verification that you haven't got a criminal record.

Professional Card

If you want to start your own business you need a professional card. You can apply for one through the Belgian embassy where your visa application is lodged, or in the commune where you live. You can approach the Ministry of Economic Affairs, and it is also worth contacting the relevant regional governments: in Brussels call 02 204 2111, in Flanders, 02 507 4367, and in Wallonia, 081 333 700.

The professional card will only be granted to businesses in a very specific field of economic activity. These businesses may also be subject to acceptance within a relevant, usually strictly regulated professional body (e.g. Kamer van Ambachten & Neringen/Chambre des Métiers & Négoces) organized on a provincial basis. The best source of information is the curiously named Ministry of Middle Classes.

WHERE TO LIVE

Most expatriates tend to be based in Brussels, and in the suburban towns and villages around the city. Areas like Uccle are expat magnets with their good housing and plethora of shopping and upmarket dining options. Richer locals migrate toward places like Tervuren, Kraainem, or Woluwe-St-Pierre. Thanks to its range of large supermarkets and fast-food places, Waterloo is sometimes said to be the most "Americanized" satellite town. It certainly has a cosmopolitan feel with English widely spoken and a good balance of services, but is rather a long way from central Brussels and the transport facilities leave much to be desired.

Apartments in certain city communes can be surprisingly affordable. Many of these communes have negative images and are unpopular options for accommodation. St Gilles is recovering from a bad reputation and is becoming trendy again, but Anderlecht is often thought of as an ethnic ghetto and a no-go area (which, of course, is a great exaggeration).

The communes in the capital of Brussels are officially bilingual (French and Flemish). But if you stay beyond the city limits, your choice of accommodation will affect the language you need to learn, especially if you are sending your children to local schools. If you are considering communes such as Overijse with their *à facilité* language rights, it's worth at least being aware of the linguistic tensions (See Chapter Three). If you want to get by only in English, Waterloo or Uccle are probably the most comfortable choices.

91

What Type of Accommodation?

Especially in Brussels, there is a reasonable choice of Aparthotels (short-term, apartment-style hotels) for those making short business sojourns. For longer stays, the main choice is between a house in the suburbs or an apartment in town. Unlike in the U.K., there are very few house-sharing arrangements where cheap rooms in a house are rented out. This is partly because rental fees are usually lower those that in London and because Belgian law holds anybody registered at an address liable for the debts of co-occupants. In other words, if your flatmate runs up a huge bill, the bailiffs could confiscate your property to pay for it, unless you have absolute proof that the items are your own. The rare house-sharing opportunities that are available are advertised in *The Bulletin*.

Beware of Extras

Apartments are generally cheaper than houses for obvious reasons, but whether you rent or buy, beware that apartments may have very substantial extra maintenance charges for heating, lighting, and the renovation of communal areas and elevators. If you are considering staying in the inner areas of the cities, check whether parking is available and if so, whether there's a separate charge.

RENTING VERSUS BUYING

Most Belgians themselves rent. Or if they buy, they stay put for a very long time. The reason is the very high costs of the taxes and fees involved, which even a healthy rise in property prices is highly unlikely to counterbalance. You'll have to pay property tax (about 1% of the total value), a massive 12.5% registration fee (reduced to 6% for especially small or cheap places), plus high administration fees. Even then, the buying procedure takes about four months of bureaucracy before you can move in. This can rarely be speeded up. All in all, if you're only intending to stay a couple of years, renting is probably more sensible. On the other hand, the taxes keep property prices relatively low, and if you need to borrow money to purchase your house, interest rates are low and are usually fixed for a considerable part of the mortgage period.

Buying Technicalities

Many houses are advertised for sale in local newspapers: in Brussels try *Le Soir* or *The Bulletin* or magazines like *Vlan*, *Immo Transit*, etc. Only some 30% of house sales are conducted through realtors/estate agents. Whether an agent is involved or not, all sales must go through a notary who plays a role somewhere between that of a lawyer and a tax collector. The notary arranges and witnesses the legalities, checks mortgage liabilities, and verifies ownership details, etc. The paperwork for all existing homes should be lodged at the cadastral/ *kadastraal* offices of the local commune.

It is not uncommon for buyer and seller to notarize an agreement in which the stated selling price is lower than the one actually agreed in private. The idea is to pay the rest in cash, thereby avoiding taxes on that portion of the transaction. This obviously appeals to the Belgian tax-dodging passion. But it is very dangerous for the buyer since there's no proof that the payment has been made, should the seller deny its receipt at some later date.

According to its age, location, and size, a house is officially assessed for property tax (revenue cadastral/*kadastraal inkommen*) by region (i.e. Brussels/Flanders/Wallonia). This represents approximately 1% of the total value, or the income that you would receive if you had rented it out (rent minus typical costs). Whether you rent your house out or not, you must add this sum to your annual declared income and pay tax on it.

Note that there are state subsidies for renovating houses of more than 15 years old, mainly in the form of tax payback on materials and labor.

Renting Technicalities

As with renting anywhere, you'll be expected to pay a deposit before moving in. This is usually equivalent to around three months rent and is paid into a dual signature account so that neither you nor the landlord can remove it without negotiation. One key thing to note is that the tenant is liable for any damage to the interior of a rented property. This includes disasters like fires or gas explosions, so to avoid the possibility of being bankrupted by such a misfortune, you are strongly advised to take out a tenant's liability insurance policy. Occasionally tenants undertake major renovation work on their places to be counted against rent, but landlords can be pretty devious, so be sure to get a watertight contract if you attempt this.

The advantage of long leases are that once signed, the landlord cannot arbitrarily raise the rent in real terms. But he/she can "adjust it for inflation" to maintain the same real-term value. If you want to leave the property before the end of the lease, you should find a replacement tenant yourself or risk incurring penalties (according to the rental contract). Even at the end of your lease, unless you confirm—by registered letter three months before the termination of your contract—that you do indeed intend to leave, the law assumes you mean to extend the agreement.

A CITIZEN'S RESPONSIBILITIES

If you've got a house, you are responsible for keeping the walkway outside your residence clear. Theoretically if you don't, you could be held responsible for accidents which occur on the pavement. If you've got a garden, there are certain rules about tree height that neighbors can have enforced should your arboretum threaten to cast too much of a shadow. More importantly, you're not allowed to make noise on a Sunday (by cutting your hedge with electrical shears, felling trees, mowing the lawn, etc.). You may be surprised to see how seriously some suburban folk take this law.

DOMESTIC HELP

That Belgium is wealthy is apparent from the number of people who hire their own cleaning staff. Twenty years ago, many such workers were Portuguese and referred to colloquially as conchitas. These days, the majority of domestic workers are more likely to be Eastern Europeans. Their services are generally procured through word of mouth or small advertisement boards in supermarkets. Note that few have legal work papers. Legally, you are supposed to have insured your domestic help against any harm that may come to your them while on your premises.

An alternative to expensive laundry services for busy people, is to find an ironing lady who will smarten up your washing once you've pulled it out of your washing machine. These folks too are likely to be working illegally, so won't necessarily advertise.

The members of the manual professions—plumbers, electricians, and handymen—are stars of the national sport of tax evasion. Everyone knows someone who can provide just what you need at a remarkable price, although you could always pay the full rate and call a bona fide company!

UTILITIES

There are many different companies supplying water, electricity, and other utility services but there is usually only one option per sector in any particular area.

Where there are choices, readers wanting the latest reviews of the services should refer to the magazine *Test Achats* (the equivalent of the British *Which?*). Water quality is excellent, usage is metered.

RUBBISH COLLECTION

Most communes organize their own systems of refuse disposal. In some you pay a fixed rate as part of local taxes, in others you have to pre-purchase special plastic sacks whose price (usually around 25BEF) includes the collection fee. Garbage collectors in the latter will ignore non-regulation bags. Often, they will not even deign to collect regulation bags if you don't place them conveniently on the pavement outside your house. You would not be the first to think of simply dumping your rubbish along a quiet street, in a public bin, or across the boundary line of a commune where collection is free. However, such behavior is illegal, and there are roving rubbish inspectors with the unpleasant chore of scrabbling through your waste. They look for telltale clues such credit card receipts or addressed envelopes that identify the offender's address. Fines start at several thousand BEF.

There are days where "special" trash is collected. The commune will post you a color-coded schedule of which days you can leave what. Read the schedule carefully as there are often a number of rules for each collection. In my commune, collections include (on different days) paper for recycling, furniture, wood and garden waste, plastics, cans and drinks cartons, and, in early January, Christmas trees! The night before the rare furniture-trash days, there's a constant trickle of vans cruising the neighborhood looking for valuable or at least re-sellable items. Dumpsites are usually authorized by the commune and you may be required to give your address as proof of residency before unloading your waste.

As in most developed countries, there are bottle banks for recy-cling glass. But note that many types of bottles (some wine, most beer) can be taken back to the store for a refund. This is generally done in supermarkets by feeding the empties into a machine at the store's entrance which adds up the total value of the glass deposited, then issues a receipt ticket which can be reimbursed at the cash registers.

TELEPHONE AND INTERNET
Unlike in the U.S., there is a per minute charge for local phone calls, and a minimum per call charge of around 5BEF. The per minute rates are somewhat lower for calls to internet providers. Belgian mobile phones follow the usual GSM standard. There are three main provid-

ers: Proximus, Mobistar, and Orange. When you are making a telephone call, note that from 2000, all numbers including the city code should be dialled, even when you're within that town.

Pay Phones

Except at stations and airports, pay phones are few and far between and relatively rarely take coins. If you find a box that does take coins, there's a 20BEF minimum call fee. Most public telephones take credit cards or pre-paid phonecards which you can buy at kiosks, train stations, and newsagents. If you have a bank card with an attached Proton electronic purse (see page 95) you can conveniently charge your card with credit in most Belgacom phone booths and then use the Proton credits to call (minimum only 10BEF per call).

Toll Numbers

There is a range of special toll rate telephone prefixes. Some important ones to be aware of include:

0800	toll free
078	1BEF/min off peak, 2BEF/min peak
070	3.5BEF/min off peak, 7BEF/min peak
077	18BEF/min: adults only, mostly for pornographic and chat-line services
0900	18BEF/min
0902	30BEF/min
0903	45BEF/min
0908/9	Variable but can be up to 90BEF/min and with a fixed dial up charge of as much as 1000BEF!

Belgacom can block calls to toll numbers. Blocking 077 calls is free, but they will charge you 605BEF plus an annual 105BEF for blocking the various options that start with the numbers 090.

Internet Service Providers

In the last year or two, free internet access has finally become available in Belgium (you still have to pay for the telephone connection). In March 2000, *Test Achats* rated Skynet as the best overall provider, and Wanadoo, the best free provider.

POST

Deliveries in Belgium are usually made only once daily during normal work hours and not at all during weekends, though collections are made on Saturday mornings.

If you are sending a letter, beware that the Belgian post office strictly enforces size and shape norms. Thus, a letter that is too big, too small, or simply an unusual shape is likely to incur a hefty premium. When shopping for Christmas cards, take with you one of the letter size templates as many British and American designed cards are the wrong dimensions.

If you're sending parcels heavier than 10 kg (approximately 22 pounds) abroad, you may find it considerably cheaper to send the contents as two smaller parcels: 10 kg is the cut off between the small package rate and the more expensive "kilopost."

For international letters, post clerks will assume you want to pay the faster *prioritaire* rate unless you state otherwise. It is important to attach the little blue *prior* airmail sticker on your letters to ensure that you actually get that faster service. There is, however, a second-class airmail (*non prioritaire*) rate. This saves just a couple of BEF on EU mail but virtually halves the cost to Australia, Japan, and North America. A small packet that I sent thus to Japan arrived in barely two weeks.

BUSINESS MATTERS

Banking and Money

Belgium has a plethora of banks, though reduced over the last three years by a rash of merges. Banking hours are not standardized, but those which open on Saturday mornings may take one afternoon off in the middle of the week. Many but not all banks close for lunch, typically from 1 to 2:30 p.m.

Opening a bank account is extremely straightforward. You will need some sort of identification, preferably a residence card, or otherwise, a passport. Most banks offer no significant interest on accounts and there may be charges associated with the statements posted to you every time there's activity on your account. A few banks, such as Argenta, do operate without bank charges and give a modest interest, but these generally don't offer the whole range of services; Argenta, for example, cannot handle foreign checks.

Debit versus Credit cards

Shops in Belgium accept the usual range of credit cards: Visa, MasterCard, AmEx, and less commonly, Diners Club. However, if you open an account, you should request a debit card (Mister Cash, Bancontact, Maestro, or the equivalent). Some supermarkets only accept debit cards. Supermarkets are usually happy to give you "cash back"—i.e. they can charge you more than your shopping bill and give you the change in cash. This is convenient and saves you the small usage charge that many account holders pay for using ATM machines. It also reduces a shop's cash holdings and the resultant risk of theft.

Proton Electronic Purse

The Proton electronic purse (e-purse) is a third type of card that is accepted in many corner shops as well as by some parking meters. Effectively this is a microchip wallet which you top up by going to an ATM or a pay phone and transferring (free of charge) a sum from your account to the card. To spend this money, a shop's card reader removes the required electronic money units from the card onto the account of the shop. This is convenient for small sums where using a credit or debit card is not economically viable. But don't load too much money at one time—if you lose the card it's like losing cash. The only way to take the credit off a Proton card is to spend it; transfers are not possible. Most Belgian debit cards now have a additional Proton function built in. Once the debit card has expired, the Proton

Most shops have terminals like these which can directly debit a customer's account (right) or take small sums from a Proton electronic purse (left). Just enter the PIN code.

card remains valid but only so long as you don't activate the replacement debit card. Go to http://load.proton.be for a demonstration on how to load your card.

Checks and Transfers

The use of personal checks in Belgium is relatively rare. A much more common method of settling bills uses the ubiquitous red and white virement/*overschrijvingsbewijf* form. For example the electricity bill might come with a pre-printed virement. You sign it, add your own account details, then drop it off at your bank. The bank will then send the requested funds to the account of the utility-provider. No need for a check, so no fear that the check will get stolen along the way. Virement forms work equally well for transferring money to friends and family if you know their account details.

MEDICINE

Belgium has one of the best health services anywhere. While health care is not entirely free in Belgium, one can choose one's doctor and seeking a second opinion is very easy and relatively inexpensive. Nor are there the infamous British delays for operations. Treatment tends to cost much less in Belgium than in the U.S. as the insurance is funneled through non-profit "mutual societies" (*mutualités*). Citizens must sign up with one such society to receive medical reimbursements from the social security system. Whatever the actual cost of treatment incurred, the state repays at the basic INAMI rate. INAMI stands for National Institute of Medical and Disability Insurance. This is almost but not quite enough to cover the cheapest option/consultation and means that those covered are not bankrupted. Note that doctors listed as *conventionné* are likely to charge fees nearest to the INAMI level and are likely to be every bit as good as private non-*conventionné* medics. Of course, the social security system only pays out for those patients who are paying contributions as an employee, officially self-employed business, or the state-funded unemployed. To top up the state system, many companies provide their employees with extra health and life insurance and a few even pay for prescription medicines which you must otherwise buy yourself. For minor afflictions, you can save a doctor's appointment and simply ask for a pharmacist's advice.

Hospitalization

If you are warded in a state or university hospital (which are perfectly good), your social security repayments will cover all but about

200BEF per day (about £3) for your accommodation charges in the cheapest rooms. If you want to save money on your medical bills, try to get yourself to the hospital. This not only saves you paying for the ambulance, but allows you to choose the cheapest option. Ambulances, in contrast, will take you to the hospital that's nearest, regardless of how high that institution's charges may be.

All patients are expected to bring their own towels, toiletries, pyjamas, etc. Note that the same taboo against serving tap water that is so visible in Belgian restaurants (See Chapter Ten) also applies in hospital; if you ask for a glass of water to wash down your pills, you'll be given (and charged for) a bottle of mineral water. There are also separate charges for using the telephone beside your bed and the TV in your room.

Medical Paperwork for Foreigners

If you are paying Belgian social security payments through your business or via your employer, you should receive the normal social security reimbursements. Non-resident visitors, especially from EU nations, often enjoy fairly comprehensive reciprocal health agreements. For example, British residents visiting Belgium need only a date-stamped E111 form which is easily obtained from a post office before leaving the U.K. and is valid for 12 months. If you need to claim, you'll need to make arrangements with a mutual society like any normal Belgian citizen, which will receive INAMI rate reimbursements on your behalf.

EDUCATION

In choosing a school for your children, you're spoilt for choice. Especially in and around Brussels, there is a wide variety of good free options within the state sector, offering education in either Flemish or French. Many have overt religious orientations. There is also a wide selection of (expensive) international schools aimed mainly at expatriates: education is possible in English, German, Japanese, and other languages around Brussels, and there are further English-language options in Antwerp and at Mons (for SHAPE employees). Brussels has an inordinate number of language schools, if you want to learn French, Flemish, or virtually any other language. And various universities offer courses in English. An invaluable reference for information about all available options is the quarterly *Newcomer* magazine or http://www.xpats.com.

Local Schools

The choice of school is up to the parents, assuming sufficient places are available. Particularly in bilingual Brussels, this is an important choice as different schools work in different languages and have specific religious affiliations. Catholic schools are often considered to offer a higher standard of education. As the system is linguistically divided, the divide between Flemish and Francophone children begins early on with little social mixing, although some enlightened parents specifically put their kids in schools of the "other" linguistic group to advance their children's bilingual prospects.

Education is mandatory until the age of 18. Belgian school kids start *gardiennes/kleutertuin* (infant school) at three and proceed to *primaires/lagereschool* (juniors) at six. When they're 12 years old, there comes the traumatic move to *humanités/middelbarschool* (secondary school) which involves a great deal more research-based study and a difficult choice of subject options.

Unlike U.K. students, school pupils in Belgium must attain a minimum standard to progress at the end of each academic year. Those who fail by a small margin are allowed to try again toward the end of the summer, by which time family holiday plans have been shot to pieces. More significant failure means re-sitting the whole year. Those failing repeatedly at *humanités* level are encouraged to seek apprenticeships or entry to a vocational school (*école supérieure/hogeschool*). which develop practical skills more than academic ones. Normally only those who complete the sixth grade of *humanités* are eligible for university, though it is technically possible to qualify by completing an extra (seventh) year of vocational school.

In principle, education is free for all registered residents, (regardless of whether you are a Belgian citizen or not). However, parents are asked to pay a series of small *frais scolaires/inschrijvingsgeld* charges (carefully itemized for photocopies, library fees, report books, school rules manual, etc.) which add up to a couple of thousand francs, twice a year. Parents are also expected to buy all school books, a list of which is presented at the beginning of each academic year (September). Textbooks can be bought secondhand at the Bourse des Livres in Brussels, ordered through the school, or (most expensively) bought from bookshops.

Schools have no personal lockers, so students have to carry around all their books for the day in big cartable bags, the designs of which make something of a fashion statement.

Discipline

In the local secondary schools, rules seem lax by my parochial standards; e.g. smoking is banned from the classroom, but openly tolerated in the school grounds. This admirable attitude adopted by the education board is supposed to make discipline less of an issue and to encourage the student to study with his/her career interests in mind. In cases where the child needs discipline, parents are frequently asked to intervene, and punishment is generally not administered by the teacher.

Parents beware. The Belgian Civil Code holds parents responsible for damage caused by the actions of their children. This was originally intended to help recoup the damages caused by teenage vandalism, but recently the law has been invoked against families of children who are disruptive at school. In one case, a family was fined 35,000BEF for failing to instil proper values in their child who was accused of taunting a fellow classmate into truancy.

Some Belgians are quick to blame recently arrived asylum seekers for behavioral problems in schools, especially recently arrived teenagers who often lack basic Flemish or French language skills. In addition, there is doubtless racism in schools, as in the rest of Belgian society, particularly toward the Turkish, North African, and Muslim minority.

Help for Parents

Belgian local schools are carefully geared to deal with working parents. Most schools have supervised drop-off facilities from 7 a.m. even though classes don't start until after 8, and similarly, schools can take care of the children for a couple of hours after the end of classes (4 p.m.) to make it possible for parents to pick them up again around 6 p.m. This pro-work attitude is also reflected in the common use of crèches. For babies three months and older, there are two types: private crèches which are expensive but usually have high supervisor to child ratios, and the cheaper, communally subsidized crèches. Forward-thinking couples are advised to book the crèche before their wedding and just hope they can produce a baby in time!

Universities

The best-known Belgian universities are at Leuven (Flemish language, founded in 1425) and Louvain-la-Neuve (French language, broke away from Leuven after the 1968 riots). For guidance with university or higher education choices, there are several helplines (e.g. 02 640 8008) and career guidance booklets (like the annual *Francophone Etudes, toutes Directions*).

The vast majority of university students study close to their parental homes and thus commute rather than live on campus. This gives many universities a rather "dead" feel in comparison to British or American colleges. Those student pads that do exist are known colloquially as *kots*. On average only 38% of those who sign up for the first year's course will make it through to the second.

Many Belgian universities have entire courses in English as do outposts of a variety of American and English universities including the Open University (tel 02 644 3368).

SHOPPING

Shops in the cities have plenty of character, there is a high concentration of delightful speciality outlets and many assistants speak surprisingly good English. The bigger supermarkets are less appealing but have products from virtually all corners of the globe, supplemented by Turkish and North African corner shops, a couple of East Asian food-stores and even a few British and American speciality shops in case you're desperate for Marmite or Hershey's chocolate.

On the other hand, don't expect to find 24-hour hypermarkets or much in the way of Sunday shopping. Supermarkets are usually open Mondays to Saturdays until 8 or 9 p.m. with most smaller businesses operating from 10 a.m. to 6:30 p.m. These smaller shops may close at lunchtime.

Markets and Sales

Markets and fairs are held regularly in town and commune squares. These usually offer high-quality fruit and vegetables, selections of cheeses and olives, barbecued meats, bargain clothes, and fake perfumes. While there are many antique shops, a good place to start your search for antiques and bric-a-bracs is the *puces* (literally fleas)/ *vlooienmarkt*, like the daily morning bric-a-brac market on Brussels' Place du Jeu de Balle. The vast majority of stuff sold here is rubbish, especially after about 6 a.m. when the dealers' buyers have passed through. But the place retains a brilliant atmosphere thanks to its Marollian characters who, by early afternoon, are selling off what's left for a few BEF a piece. The stalls in the Sablon area are a big step up in quality. There are dozens of other markets, the biggest of which jams the roads around Brussels' south station on Sundays selling virtually anything moveable. The Anderlecht abattoir holds various

various livestock markets during the week there's a horse market in Molenbeek-St-Jean on Friday mornings, and a daily plant and flower market in the Brussels Grand Place.

A *brocante/rommelmarkt* is equivalent to a British car-boot-sale —like a flea markets except that it's open to ordinary people to sell their motley selection of unwanted clothes, furniture, books and bric-a-brac. For the most popular ones (e.g. on the Carrefour/ex-Biggs car park in Waterloo every Sunday) vendors arrive before dawn to claim a valuable pitch. Often a roadside *brocante* is one feature of a village *braderie*—a kind of fête at which the town center is closed to traffic while various cafés and street sellers serve drinks and snacks on the pavements and shops offer limited discounts. This is *not*, as Belgians are swift to point out, the same as the sales (*soldes/solden*), which are legally limited to two officially designated periods in January and July. Suburban homes also run garage sales, known in Belgium as, well, garage sales.

Special Regional Products

Lace	Brussels, Bruges
Diamonds, gold, avant-garde fashion	Antwerp
Crystal glassware	Seraing
Hand-beaten copperware	Dinant

Chapter Eight

TRAVELING IN BELGIUM

Belgium is blessed with many good things. But great public transport is not one of them. Buses and trains cover most of the country but suburban services don't quite run frequently enough to really generate mass usage. Even in the city of Brussels, you may often have to wait up to 20 minutes before a metro train arrives. This encourages commuters to drive, which further reduces passenger revenues and worsens the traffic load. A vicious circle. All the more vicious considering the discourteous and dangerous Belgian driving style.

DAILY TRAFFIC CHAOS

Rush hour traffic is bad anywhere. And bus drivers' frequent strikes don't help. The Gent, Antwerp, and Brussels Ring roads often resemble car parks during rush hour. It's not unusual to see drivers reading a book at the wheel as they inch forward. The blockages are bad enough if everyone's driving sensibly. If there's a crash, the whole system comes to a standstill. And there's nowhere more likely to cause a crash than that most infamous of blackspots, the Carrefour Léonard. Here the Brussels Ring intersects the Brussels–Namur motorway with an interchange so confusing, it requires a Ph.D. to

Give way! You are always in the wrong in a tangle with a tram.

negotiate. Turning certain directions involves several perilous stops and starts while attempting to cross the oncoming streams of international juggernauts. An amusing advertisement quipped ironically "A user's manual for the Carrefour Léonard? If one exists, you'll find it in the Yellow Pages!".

Traffic is noticeably lighter (except on weekends) between July 1 and August 31, during the school holiday season. However, on Sunday evenings in summer or at the end of long weekends, the motorways back to Brussels from Ostend and from the Ardennes can be chock-full of cars.

DRIVING

Belgian driving standards are infamous. Glance at the walls of the tunnels that wind beneath each of the bigger cities and you will see that barely an inch has not been scratched and scarred by a vehicle that has lost control. Curve-barriers are repeatedly buckled from crashes, motorway tarmac is artistically adorned with skid tracks and small suburban shrubberies are felled every weekend by sozzled chauffeurs.

There was once a good reason for all this mayhem. Driving tests were only introduced in 1967. Prior to that, to get a driver's license, you simply had to go to the commune, pay a fee, and swear that you knew how to drive. A suitable hole was punched in your identification card and that was it. Off you go. Notwithstanding the better training today's drivers undergo, many still seem addicted to speeding, drink-driving, bullying pedestrians, and tailgating. When driving abroad, my wife occasionally mutters darkly at other road users, "Watch out! Don't you know there's a Belgian behind you!" And she's only half joking.

Bob Tonight?

A high-profile publicity campaign tried to persuade Belgium's notoriously merry motorists that it's sexy to be "Bob." A "Bob" (or "Bobette") stays sober to drive the rest of his (or her) friends home after a party. But most Belgians scorn drink-driving laws. There are potentially harsh penalties if you are caught driving with more than 0.5 grams of alcohol per litre of blood (ranging from on-the-spot fines of more than 12,000BEF, to the immediate confiscation of drivers' licenses and up to a year in jail). But the fact is that, few really expect to be caught. Even when they crash! Police frequently find cars abandoned and their injured drivers lurking in undergrowth to avoid the breath-test rather than seeking medical help. And I've seen cases myself where "helpful" traffic policemen simply ask about a crashed driver's welfare, apparently choosing not to notice his near paralytic condition.

Even if you are stopped by the police, you're allowed to request 30 minutes to breathe, drink water, and crunch garlic to mask the smell of alcohol before you are eventually breathalysed. The very fair-minded principle is to prevent unfairly punishing those who may have happened to have just one single drink (swigged on departure to steady the nerves for the journey?!). Even when you crash! Belgian stories are full of cases where traffic policemen are more concerned about your welfare than the cause of the accident.

There have been bizarre cases where drunk drivers, spying a police car approaching, have nimbly jumped into the back seat with their passengers. Thus, when the police officer opens the door, he finds the driver's seat empty and the back seat crammed with "hitchhikers."

If you want to be law-abiding and find yourself without a "Bob" at hand, you can still reach home drunk and in one piece with the help of a volunteer group called Responsible Young Drivers. The volunteers work in pairs; one drives you home in your own car, the other follows in a second vehicle to pick up his partner after the ride. Note, however, that they operate only on special occasions. On millennium night, the group aided some 3080 revellers in various states of intoxication. Of those who did choose to drive that night, only 10% caught were legally "intoxicated"—a score that my Belgian wife deemed suspiciously low.

Speeding
Belgian motorists seem to perceive posted speed limits as minima

rather than maxima and growl bitterly at those law-abiding slow-coaches who persist in sticking to the generally disdained limit. Things get especially dangerous in the rare but severe snows that occasionally catch the country unawares and put skates beneath those macho lorry drivers who frighteningly consider their trucks immune to skidding.

The chances of being caught for speeding may be higher than for boozing. But that is not saying much. Radar guns may be used without you ever noticing—until the fine notice turns up in the mail. The police tell radio stations where many of the speed traps are for each day. And radio stations make regular bulletins. So as long as you listen carefully, you can continue to drive like a maniac almost anywhere else! The possible logic for divulging the speed guns' positions is delightfully Belgian. Radio stations can't be prevented from divulging such information—there's a free press. And motorists who spot a radar trap might phone in reports to radio stations on mobile phones. But such phones are illegal and dangerous to use while driving. So why not be safe and simply have the gendarmerie announce the trap locations in the first place.

Pedestrian Crossings

There are two types of pedestrian crossings. Neither are entirely safe. Those color-coded with red and green lights are the better of the two. But many show the "green-man" symbol while turning traffic is simultaneously allowed to filter around the corners: straight into the pedestrians' path. So watch very carefully. Then there are the "normal" crossings: thick (if tellingly faded) black and white stripes painted across the street and marked on the roadside by a blue triangular sign. Legally pedestrians have the right of way to cross here. But believe that at your mortal peril. It is a relatively new rule, and the stream of traffic is unlikely to even slow down for you. If you stride forth confidently asserting your rights (as one would on a British zebra crossing), most drivers will simply look at you with a mixture of bemusement and annoyance as they try to knock you down.

Driving instructors are in a quandary over these crossings. Since the correct (if rarely observed) rule says that drivers *should* stop for pedestrians, learner drivers ought, theoretically, to be so taught. The problem is that practising the manoeuvre is dangerous for student and instructor alike. Driving schools claim it's their major cause of crashes: the drivers behind simply don't expect anyone to stop for pedestrians, so slam straight into the back of the practice car.

Priorité à Droite

As if all the other dangers weren't enough, traffic on Belgian roads has the extra challenge of observing the suicidal French-style *priorité à droite* rule. This gives the right of way to a vehicle shooting out from the right rather than to the stream of traffic going straight ahead. The rule makes sense at the unmarked junction of two roads of similar sizes. But when a tiny country lane joins a big thoroughfare, the potential for disaster is obvious. It is compounded by the caveat that you lose the priority should you slow to a halt. Thus to maintain the right to advance, it's important not to watch where you're going. Silly? So it would seem to most visitors. And in private many Belgians quietly admit that *priorité à droite* is a well-intentioned but potentially lethal anachronism. But God help any foreigner who criticizes it: you may be seen as making a cultural attack, rubbing salt into an open wound, or, at best, being boringly predictable.

Note that not all roads are ruled by *priorité à droite*. You can relax en route stretches with occasional yellow-on-white diamond roadside signs. And if you see a row of triangular white "teeth" painted across your path at a junction, you must give way—even if you are advancing from the right. Finally, at a roundabout (rotary) the vehicle going around the circle has priority over another vehicle approaching from a side road. That is normal the world over, isn't it? Yes. But beware. In Belgium, the opposite was true until very recently. And some drivers are a little forgetful.

Buying Cars

Belgium was once one of the cheapest places in Europe to buy new cars, though recently the advantages have been whittled away to virtually nil. Belgians themselves show an extraordinary enthusiasm for the Salon de l'Auto car show held every two years at the Heysel exhibition grounds in Brussels. Some car brands take as much as 40% of their annual order during the fair, which draws a phenomenal 10% of the national population each time! Besides the fair, there is the usual network of dealers (bargain hard!) and you can get a price guide from *Auto Gids* or *Moniteur de l'Automobile*. For second-hand cars check the fortnightly Auto-Occasion. Note that unlike the U.K., it's usually better to sell a car second-hand than to trade it in with a dealer, though either way, prices are pretty low.

Even the most comprehensive Belgian automobile insurance scheme may not cover the loss of a car's contents. And it's very wise to get legal defence liability coverage too. Insurance normally covers the car rather than the driver.

Number Plates

In Belgium, license plates are registered to a driver not a car (except for company or commercial vehicles). The front number plate is simply a copy that the owner has made at a key-cutting store but the back plate has security markings and a fluorescent backing. It's the back plate that carries all the legal importance, so stealing it from a car is an extremely cruel practical joke which can cause months of bureaucratic difficulties for the owner and is almost worse than having the whole car taken.

Private plates have red characters on a white background. CD in green letters on an otherwise ordinary plate means the driver has diplomatic immunity, so keep out of his/her way! They won't be responsible if they crash into you.

If a lad turns up on a date in a flashy Ferrari, he is much less likely to impress the girl if the license plates are in green letters. She'll assume that his dad is a car salesman; such plates are for cars held by the dealer awaiting a buyer.

White letters on a red plate indicate a car "in transit," i.e. bought here but destined for export. The owners of these cars may avoid the 21% VAT, but the car must be exported within a year.

Blue letters on white plates with the EU symbol denote the number plates of cars driven by those who work at the EU. The plates give certain preferential parking possibilities to Eurocrats who are mostly expatriates with large, tax-free salaries. The result is a certain degree of resentment from ordinary Belgians, beaten at their own national sport of tax-avoidance. Thus, drivers of cars bearing blue plates suffer the same nagging insecurities as wearers of fur coats in London.

Petrol

Service stations may not sell petrol above an officially announced maximum price per litre, though several (such as Octa+) regularly charge less. Changes in this official price are announced on the evening news almost daily.

On weekends or late evenings, many garages appear to be closed but in fact you can often still use the petrol pumps and make payment with a debit card or by putting a 1000BEF note into a self-service slot. If a Belgian finds himself anywhere near Luxembourg, he/she will naturally be tempted to detour through the Grand-Duchy to fill the tank virtually tax free.

TAXIS

In taxis as in restaurants, there is absolutely no compunction to tip. The gratuity is already included in the quoted fare, though this doesn't stop certain drivers trying to persuade you otherwise. Taxi fares can usually be paid by credit card in the car. In Brussels, the minimum charge is 95BEF (170BEF at night) plus 38BEF/km and 10BEF/minute waiting time (which includes travel at under 15 km/h). You should note that the rate doubles if you want to travel beyond city limits (e.g. to the airport, which is in Zaventem).

TRAIN—SNCB/NMBS

Belgium is reputed to have the densest railway network in the world. The Brussels–Mechelen line was the first on the European continent to run a passenger service. These days, services are moderately priced and run at hourly intervals on most routes. At main stations, departure boards are usually clearly marked but remember that place names look different in French and Flemish. When reading timetables, note that yellow posters quote departures while white ones are for arrivals. There are quite different but similar looking timetables for weekdays, and for weekends or holidays.

There are weekend specials and "B-excursion" tickets which may include the entrance fee to an event or attraction. For major events such as the carnival at Binche or the Ros Beiaardommegang in Dendermonde, return tickets to the site are sold at a major (60%) reduction to encourage drivers to leave their cars behind. For very special events, Belgian railways sometimes get generous and give away tickets, as they did for the wedding of Prince Philip on December 4, 1999. Strangely, you could get a pair of free tickets from anywhere to anywhere, not just to Brussels to see the spectacle. So rather than watch the wedding, Belgians left the capital en masse for a free weekend at the seaside! The B-Tourrail offers the best deal: free travel anywhere within the country for five stated days within a one-month period for only around 2280BEF (about 3500BEF for first class). There are also special deals for people over 60 years old and for big families (very Catholic!). You can find out more by visiting the website http://www.b-rail.be/.

Belgium has at least two seasonal steam railways: Trois Vallées (Treignes to Mariembourg in Hainaut, April–Oct only) and Vennbahn (Eupen to Robertville, a few weekends per year).

At Brussels Airport Le Chat welcomes you and bids farewell all in one breath.
Note the use of English with French and Flemish translations relegated below!

BUSES AND TRAMS

Belgium has three main public bus companies: STIB/MIVB for Brussels (which also operates the capital's tram and metro system), De Lijn for Flanders (literally The Line) and Transport en Commun (TEC) for Wallonia. Bus frequency on many routes diminishes considerably at weekends. Brussels and certain other cities have fairly extensive streetcar networks but be careful when driving near or across the tracks: If a tram hits you, it is always considered "your fault." The Brussels Tramway Museum shows off a great variety of trams which are mostly still in working order and, on special occasions, are still used as public transport. An intriguing way to celebrate is to rent out a party-tram and driver from STIB (evenings and weekends only, up to 40 revellers per tram).

CYCLING AND RAMBLING

In the provinces, particularly Flanders, there are extensive cycle paths and sign-posted hiking trails. You can rent mountain bikes at certain railway stations and many tourist offices provide fairly detailed walking and cycling maps to help you explore the area. Attractive VTT (mountain bike) trails are also found in the Ardennes. However, on the busy city streets of Brussels, cycling approximates to attempted suicide. This is ironic considering the popularity of the sport of cycle racing (See Chapter Twelve). Roadside cycle paths in the suburbs frequently end suddenly or slam into high kerbs. Drivers have no more respect for cyclists than they do for pedestrians, and are highly unlikely to grant priority to cycle lanes even where they are legally supposed to. If you have a bike (or indeed a horse) in Brussels, the best place to ride it is the glorious Forêt de Soignes, through a cathedral of beech trees with miles of peaceful bridle paths and cycle tracks. And no cars.

If you want to buy a bike, there are plenty of specialist but pricey bicycle shops. The hypermarkets sometimes have great deals on bicycles but usually stock only a limited range of sizes which may come in a box, making it rather difficult to test ride before you buy. You can buy a secondhand bicycle at a special market on the Blvd du Midi/Zuidlaad near the Brussels Midi/Zuid station (Sunday 7 a.m. to 2 p.m.) or through small ads like those posted on http://www.xpats.com.

WATER TRANSPORT

While canals in Britain have been largely relegated to servicing pleasure cruise holiday-makers, in Belgium waterways still carry significant industrial cargoes and receive major investment. Huge vessels of up to 9000 tonnes can reach Liège via the Albert canal. The curious inclined lock at Ronquières, like a massive bath on wheels, allows sizeable barges to reach Charleroi from Antwerp. And the brand new rotating hydraulic lift at Strépy-Thieu has been built to expedite heavy boat traffic between the Rhine, Scheldt/Escaut, and Maas/Meuse rivers.

Despite the major industrial traffic, several sections of Belgian waterways are accessible to pleasure boats. Tourists seem to love the Damme–Bruges paddleboat run. An appealing 21 km (13 miles) of the Lesse between Anseremme and Dinant have been set aside for kayaking, and there are summer rides between the rocks and trees down the Semois from Chiny (by reservation, call 09 554 9372).

GOING ABROAD

Airlines

The Belgian national airline is Sabena. Once nicknamed "Such A Bad Experience, Never Again," its image has improved in recent years. It serves an impressive range of African destinations, as well as covering almost all of Europe in its partnership with Swissair and the Qualiflyer group. However, 2001 has been a terrible year for the airline and it teeters on the edge of bankruptcy as we go to press. No frills Brussels-based Virgin Express operates Sabena code-share routes to Barcelona, Madrid, Milan, Rome, Nice, and London Heathrow with tickets generally cheaper and booked direct (call 02 752 0505). The absolute cheapest fares to London are on Ryanair (web promotional offers as incredibly low as 100BEF + tax to Stanstead) which also serves Venice-Treviso, Pisa, Carcassonne, Glasgow-Prestwick, Dublin, and Shannon all from its new local hub at Charleroi (sometimes misleadingly referred to as "Brussels South"). See the Resource Guide for website details. Other Belgian airlines include VLM (Antwerp to London City or Geneva), Sobelair (Sabena's charter-airline), and CityBird (long-haul charters). Super-fast Thalys trains direct from Brussels and Antwerp to both Schiphol (Amsterdam) and Charles de Gaule (Paris) airports mean passengers have an increasingly wide range of long-haul options.

Travel Agencies

USIT Connections and Airstop/Taxistop are the most prominent travel agencies each with an e-mail service which can alert you to cheap deals and student and discount tickets. See the Resource Guide chapter for details.

The Last Call shop within Brussels Airport provides absolute last-minute tickets. They take no telephone calls. You just turn up between 6 and 7 a.m. with your bags packed and hope for tickets to your desired destination. Or go wherever's cheapest! Prices quoted are for return trips with minimum one weekend stay, maximum one month.

Getting to the Airports

You can reach Brussels Airport by express trains that leave four times an hour from Brussels Midi/Zuid via Brussels Central and North stations. If you are traveling by road, use the dauntingly large but feebly signposted intersection 4 off the Brussels Ring, following the minuscule signs for "Zaventem." If you're planning to do this any time near rush hour, add an hour or more in anticipation of the traffic chaos.

Antwerp Airport is located in Deurne, 5 km by bus number 16 from the Antwerpen Centraal station. Charleroi Airport is served by bus number 68 from Charleroi Sud station (one to two buses per hour) and by Ryanair buses from outside the Wild Geese Irish pub in Brussels (Metro Maalbeek).

To or from Belgium by Land

High speed Thalys, Eurostar, and TGV train services link Brussels to Amsterdam and Paris, London, and even Marseille (in little more than five hours). Tickets for those services must be booked ahead but are available from railway stations, which also sell cheaper inter-city tickets to the same and many other destinations. Eurolines buses offer a range of international services from outside Brussels North railway station and also from Liège, Gent, Antwerp, and Kortrijk. There are several smaller international bus companies: look around Brussels Midi/Zuid Station for companies serving Spain and Morocco, and behind the Central Station where the buses bound for Eastern Europe park. Another cheap way to travel to European destinations is with a car-share which pairs long-distance drivers with passengers who pay per kilometer. With Airstop/Taxistop's "Eurostop" scheme you give 1BEF/km to the driver plus pay an additional 0.3BEF/km fee for the arrangement (tel 02 223 2310). Slightly cheaper is the "Service Lift" arranged through Brussels' Radio 21 station (also 1BEF/mile but no fee). However, the latter operates only during academic holiday periods. The information on the destinations served is read out daily on 99.1FM and listed on RTBF TV teletext page 580. Or call 02 737 2021.

Chapter Nine

CHIPS, CHOCOLATE, AND MUSSELS

Brits with long memories may remember *Not the Nine O'Clock News*—a partly topical comedy show in the early 1980s. And one which, curiously, has enjoyed recent repeats on Flemish TV. In one sketch a pre-Mr Bean Rowan Atkinson played the Belgian cultural attaché asked to explain cultural nuances that Belgians used to express their appreciation of their food. The hilarious if utterly untrue answers included gratuitous farting and burping and culminated in the question, "But what if you wanted to say, 'that's the best meal I've ever tasted'?" Answer? "Not a very likely contingency...in Belgium." Across the U.K., people roared with laughter.

Clearly very few viewers had actually eaten in Belgium. The collective assumption that "Belgian = boring = bad food" couldn't be further from the truth. Belgians love to eat out. And a relatively wealthy, demanding clientele actually supports a very high quality and competitive *restauration* trade (See Chapter Ten).

These days the world is better informed. One internet site gushes accurately, if inelegantly that gastronomically, Belgium is "not the sleepy sister of France; it's a chowhound Mecca". The establishment of the Belgo restaurant chain (since 1992) has helped to change images, as do all the Euroland expatriates returning happily over-weight. The taste for luxury is emphasized at Christmas: while the English-speaking world stuffs its turkey, and the Eastern Europeans choose their carp, wealthier Belgians are off to the supermarket to collect their box-full of pre-ordered lobsters.

French visitors are frequently surprised to find that French food in Brussels restaurants and bakeries is consistently better and of better value than in much of France. Day-to-day home-cooked meals may be less inspired "meat-and-two-veg" variants, but are typically rich and hearty offering few compromises to the concerns of dieticians. Beyond the evils of the Brussels sprout, Belgium's most famous contributions to gastronomy—chocolate, chips, and mussels—reflect its international flavor. After all potatoes and cocoa are New World products while the best "Belgian" mussels are usually imported from the town of Yerseke, just across the Dutch border.

AT THE BAKERY

Belgian bakers reckon they make French bread better than the French. Sounds like an oxymoron. Yet on the whole, I agree. And it's not just the *pains Français* (baguettes): Belgian bread comes in all shapes and

123

sizes. Sliced bread is popular. The slicing is performed to order by the baker, who'll usually charge a couple of BEF for the service and paper bag. In supermarkets, you'll have to slice it yourself. This means confronting a machine which looks like it belongs in a medieval dungeon. Put the loaf in through the flap in the rear section and close the door. Press the green button. A whirring of electric saws begins and the loaf starts to emerge from the set of metal teeth. Once the bread has escaped, place it onto the angular metal tongue on the top of the contraption to make bagging it up more straightforward.

What's What in a Baker's Shop

Fresh bread should be available most of the day, but toward closing time the choice is considerably diminished. *Couques* such as croissants and *pain au chocolat* are usually available only in the mornings.

Most *boulangerie/patisserie* shops have a wide range of cakes and other temptations on offer including a selection of chocolates and tarts. *Tarte au sucre/zuikertort* is caramelized sugar in an open pastry base. There are also a wide variety of fruit pies such as the classic Walloon *tarte aux groseilles vertes* (gooseberry tart). Arguably, some of the country's best tarts come from a small roadside *tarterie* in the tiny township of Chaumont-Gistoux, southeast of Wavre. People making the considerable drive from Brussels don't seem to mind the lengthy wait and curt service they get from the shop attendants.

The following are some other morsels you can find at a bakery:

pains à la Grecque	neither Greek nor bread, this Belgian biscuit is a trademark of the venerable 1829 Dandoy *patisserie* at 31 rue au Beurre, Brussels
pain au chocolat (French)	croissant with chocolate filling (*chocolade broodje* in Flemish)
pistolets (French)	not small guns but small, round bread rolls
achtje (Flemish)	literally means eight in Flemish, but in *patisserie* terms, these are pastries moulded into the figure of eight with a custard paste in each lobe
kaasflap (Flemish)	cheese turnover
kersengebak (Flemish)	small cherry tarts
rozijnkoek (Flemish)	fruit cake

suikerwafel (Flemish)	sugar waffle
worstenbrood (Flemish)	sausage roll

Bakery-coffee Shops

The coffee that you can expect in most Belgian bakery-coffee shops will be of espresso strength and usually served with a wrapped square of chocolate or a *speculoos*. The latter is like a sculpted ginger nut without the ginger, semi-sweet and hard enough that it doesn't sag if dunked. Special Santa-shaped *speculoos* are presented to children on St Nicolas Day. Unlike in France, you don't have to ask for or pay for milk or creamer with your coffee. This comes automatically in a small jug or a plastic tub. Beware that many cafés consider a "cappuccino" to be coffee smothered with whipped cream rather than with added steamed milk as you might be expecting. Many coffee houses are attached to bakeries, so you can sit and enjoy their pastries too, albeit at slightly higher than off-the-shelf prices.

Traiteurs and Sandwich Bars

Belgian delicatessens (*traiteurs*) offer a wide range of cooked meats and pre-prepared gourmet meals, as well as a selection of salads and sandwich fillers. A sandwich = *belegd broodje* in Flemish. Popular as a quick working lunch, the assistant will cut and fill half a baguette to order for around 80–100BEF.

CHEESE

Sandwiched between the great cheese producers, France and Holland, Belgium's brands are relatively unknown. Yet some 300 cheeses are produced. The most celebrated is the infamously smelly Herve, the recognized appellation protégé from, well, Herve. If you are curious about the cheese, visit Herve in late October, when it holds its cheese and wine fair. Also much touted are the abbey cheeses, many of which are produced by the same religious institutions who turn out the famous beers (to which the cheeses make an ideal accompaniment). Chimay makes one variety incorporating the beer into the recipe. Gent's *pas de bleu*, the first Belgian blue cheese, is somewhat similar to a Stilton. *Aux orties* cheeses are flecked with what appear to be herbs but are in fact crushed, dried stinging nettles.

On the second last Sunday of August, don't be alarmed if you see men who look curiously like gnomes in their traditional blue and red costumes wheeling around huge slabs of creamy, white-skinned Passendale cheeses piled upon black, low-slung barrows on the streets. The spectacle before you is the Passendale's biennial cheese parade. You can sample a wider range of Belgian cheeses at the National Belgian Cheese Festival, which is held on the last weekend of August in Harzé Castle (tel 087 679 845 for details).

CHOCOLATE

Belgians eat almost 8 kg (18 pounds) of chocolate per person per year. Given the vast selection available, one might imagine that the figure was even higher. Mini bars provide temptation at supermarket checkouts, many Belgian homes stash a slab of Côte d'Or for a sly nibble and chocolate fingers or individually wrapped squares are de rigueur for coffee-dunking. But for gifts or treats, locals visit the specialist chocolate shops that line local high streets in economically improbable numbers. Belgians refer to their top quality, individually filled, bite-sized chocolates as *pralines*, though these need not strictly be praline- (i.e. ground hazelnut) flavored. The term was coined in 1912 in honor of the early chocoholic Comte de Praslin. The Swiss grandfather of their creator, Belgian chocolatier Jean Neuhaus, had set up shop in Brussels' glorious Galeries Royales St Hubert in 1857. The boutique is still there.

Chocolate Controversies

The subject of chocolate is a matter of national pride and can raise a surprising degree of emotion amongst the masses as the following examples reveal:

Côte d'Or

Established in 1883, Côte d'Or became Belgium's dominant mass market brand, equivalent to Cadbury in the U.K. or Hershey in the United States, though Belgians would balk at the comparison. When the company was sold to the multinational conglomerate Kraft Jacobs Suchard, the sense of national loss was akin to that felt in Britain over the sale of the Rolls Royce Car company.

What is Chocolate Anyway?

The political wrangling over this technical definition may sound silly, but in Belgium, the issue is major news. The problem is that the EU definition and the traditional Belgian definitions are different. Until recently, the Belgians could only call their product chocolate if it used 100% cocoa butter. Now the EU has decided, in its fallible wisdom, that the exact meaning of the term chocolate should be standardized across the Union. After pressure from the U.K. industry where manufacturers customarily dilute their cocoa butter, this definition will henceforth allow chocolate-makers to use up to 5% vegetable fats in their products. However, many Belgian producers claim they will retain the old standard.

Belgian Chocolates: Types and Tips

Pralines (fancy chocolates) are sold by weight in attractive mini-boxes fastened with ribbons. In these shops one is faced with a choice that's as bewildering as that for a first-timer in an American coffee shop. You can select the varieties that take your fancy, or save the bother by choosing a pre-packed assortment.

The following main types are on offer:

Manons	usually have a chocolate outer shell, and a fresh cream center. They are best eaten within a few days of purchase.
Gianduja	my personal favorites. These are extremely smooth mixtures of chocolate, icing sugar, and finely powdered nut. Commonly sold in little bars wrapped in gold paper.
Ganache	the mainstay of the industry. *Ganache* is a smooth mix of chocolate and *crème fraîche*. Often used as a filling with various crunchy ingredients.
Truffles	are ball-shaped *ganaches*, often with a hardened coat dusted in cocoa powder. Especially popular around Christmastime and often sold in small stalls at seasonal markets.

All types should be kept reasonably cool and dry, but not in a fridge.

Which Brand to Choose?

In choosing chocolates for gifts, there is a somewhat defined hierarchy of perceived qualities which is reflected in the price and the appropriateness of a specific brand. For myself or anyone abroad I'd buy Leonidas—dream-like quality at great prices. But to impress a Belgian I'd have to pay almost double and go for brands like Godiva, Corné, or Neuhaus. There are also many smaller family chocolatier brands. Some, like Wittamer, will prove very successful presents, but the choice should be very carefully made, especially if you're buying a business gift.

MEAT AND MEAT ATTITUDES

Belgians like their meat and are not afraid of blood. "Medium" steaks are served red. Rare ones walk away by themselves. Meat ordered "blue" is simply warmed rather than cooked. *Filet Américain* is frequently a disappointment to visitors from the United States who unwittingly assume it's a quaint term for hamburger or steak. In fact it's raw minced beef, known in France as steak tartare. *Carpaccio*, Italian-style slices of raw beef make a popular and very acceptable starter when doused in parmesan cheese and olive oil.

Belgians are not sentimentally squeamish over Black Beauty either, and horse-meat is a traditional favorite: pony steak is said to be tender while steeplechase horses are reputed to have the best taste. Traditionally horse butchers ran niche shops, but although at least one remains in Charleroi, such specialist shops are increasingly rare. It's not that animal lovers are prevailing. These days, tastes are just getting even more exotic. No major modern supermarket is complete without springbok, crocodile, llama, etc. Ostrich steaks are slowly becoming accepted as rather superior to steak for tender, velvety red meat. Winter is the season for game which features not just pheasant, duck, and venison, but also wild boar. In French, there are two terms for boar meat: *sanglier* is the strongly flavored meat from the full grown beast while *marcassin* is from the milder tasting young.

Boudins are various varieties of sausage, not unique to Belgium but much appreciated. A *boudin noir* is a blood and pork fat sausage a little like black pudding. *Boudin blanc* is filled with stuffing and white poultry and other varieties add to this herbs, spinach, vegetables, and/or raisins. Small versions—some in spicy or curry flavors—are popular in summer barbecues. A plate of black and white boudin is known collectively as "Sky and Earth" as the dish would originally have been served with mashed potatoes (the "earth") and stewed apple (from "heaven above"). *Boudin* in Francophone slang can also be equated to the English insult, fat slag, a less than flattering term for an overweight, meretricious female.

Vegetarians and Animal Rights

Vegetarian restaurants are few and far between and "animal rights" viewpoints are far from universally appreciated. There is a Belgian Animal Liberation Front which has very occasionally attacked fast-food outlets like McDonalds and the homegrown burger chain Quick. The Ardennes is the homeland of the St Hubert Foundation which actively promotes game hunting and backs it up by providing New Year's dinners of fresh wild boar for the homeless in Luxembourg Province. Protesters against the consumption of veal calves are widely assumed to be weirdos who don't like drinking milk (of which veal is simply an economic side product). Most Belgians will happily nibble garlic-plastered frogs' legs unconcerned at how they were severed from the frogs. And they are unashamedly proud to serve the ultimate animal-lovers' taboo: *foie gras*, (the smooth liver of force-fed geese) washing away any qualms with a sweet Sauternes.

VEGETABLES

In medieval times, most of the peasant population survived on a diet of cabbage and beet pottage. Thus, cabbage entered the European psyche where it has lodged for centuries: babies were supposed to arrive in a cabbage leaf—stork assisted or otherwise—and cabbage soup was traditionally served to Belgian newlyweds the morning after their marriage.

In the 13th century, a group of Belgian farmers committed what is for me the culinary equivalent of crime against humanity: they developed the Brussels sprout (*chou de Bruxelles/spruitje*). Braised by the best chefs or smothered Belgian-style with butter, nutmeg, and onion, I have an irrational horror of these mini-cabbages. Fortunately Brussels sprouts are not that popular. In fact, the most archetypal Belgian vegetable is something altogether different: the endive.

Endives

Known in Belgium as *chicons/witloof*, the nation has an inexplicable enthusiasm for these hand-sized yellow-white vegetables which look like gigantic rosebuds sucked pallid by a vegetarian vampire. Their discovery is ascribed to a careless 1830s Schaerbeek farmer by the name of Antonius Dekoster. He had been storing chicory roots intended for use as a coffee additive. He left them too long, however, and the roots started to germinate. Nibbling at the buds, he found them surprisingly tasty. Their deliberate production was undertaken by a botanist called Brézier who started marketing them in 1846.

There are three main Belgian preparations of endives: raw in salads, coarsely sliced and fried in butter, then served as a vegetable side dish, or, most notably, rolled in ham and baked whole in a calorie-packed cheese sauce.

White Asparagus

There's considerable demand for this homegrown delicacy, dubbed "white gold" by those who promote it. Generally white asparagus is only in season from May to June.

SEAFOOD

A Craving for Crustacea

Belgians enjoy a great variety of prawn lookalikes, from the Christmas lobster to the decorative *écrevisse via gambas*, *crevettes géantes*, *langoustines*, and scampi. The most popular of all are surely the home produced North Sea *crevettes grises*, or in direct translation, grey shrimps. Smaller and less visually attractive than their bigger pink cousins, they are nonetheless much tastier and more expensive. Fried in a parsley, cheese, and cream croquette or stuffed into hollowed-out tomatoes, grey shrimps represent a little niche of Belgian culinary heaven. The minuscule creatures are traditionally collected by artisan

No carving is necessary for this Belgian Christmas dinner.

crevettiers around Ostend. At Oostduinkerke, *crevettiers* still ride horseback through shallow waters, trawling for the little critters during the shrimp-catching festival which takes place in late June.

Moules/Mosselen/Mussels

Moules frites (mussels and chips) is about as Belgian as food gets. Belgians expect big, succulent, carefully de-bearded mussels which put to shame the piffling gritty minnows served in restaurants in some other countries. During mussel season (usually July–March), supermarkets sell hundreds of pounds of the live shellfish together with packets of the diced onions, celery, and herbs you need to make the required broth cooking-base. Then it's up to you to add your choice of beer, wine, garlic, etc. to the boiling pot. Then, the mussels are served, shells and all, in a steaming casserole dish. To eat, simply take the shell of the first mussel you attack to act as tweezers for eating the rest. Don't try to force a mussel that doesn't open easily; it was probably dead before cooking and won't do you any good.

The classic chain of restaurants for mussels is Chez Léon. But mussels are also ubiquitous on menus even in motorway service areas and supermarket cafeterias. Usually the accompanying fries are *à volonté* (eat as many as you like).

Fish

If you're choosing a fish menu to impress the Belgian sense of snobbery, the best choice is monkfish (*lotte/zeeduivel*). In the Ardennes, trout (*truite/forel*) is a speciality. *Truite au bleu* is trout served with carrots, leeks, and potatoes and is not blue at all. However the traditional Flemish "eel in green" (*Paling in 't groen/anguilles au vert*) is about as green as it can get thanks to a rich sorrel sauce. The most appealing, typically Belgian fish dish is probably *waterzooï*. Alternatively made using chicken, it's a classic meal in a bowl—somewhere between a creamy stew and a rich, thick soup with chunks of vegetable and potatoes. Fish dishes served *à l'Escavèche* come in a vinegar marinade. *Saurets/bokking* are salty, smoked herring, not as dry as kippers, and sold un-filleted in brown and white varieties.

Fishy French Slang

Maquereau (mackerel) and *morue* (cod) appear on menus, but, in a different context, are terms in colloquial French used to denote pimps and prostitutes respectively. A *merlan* (whiting) is more innocuous: to "make eyes like a fried whiting" means to roll your eyes. The slang usage of a single mussel (*moule*) is anatomically feminine and simply too rude to utter in public, so always play it safe and refer to mussels in the plural!

TRADITIONAL BELGIAN CUISINE

One of the delights of getting beneath the skin of a culture is learning about the ordinary day-to-day foods that most people traditionally ate—and often still do. Beneath the fine dining Belgian sophistication, lies the potato-mash of everyday reality. Some of the most archetypal Belgian meals simply don't feature on restaurant menus.

Boulettes/Ballekes

For Belgians, the gastronomic skeleton in the kitchen cupboard is undoubtedly *ballekes*. Traditionally, the quality of her *ballekes* was said to be the measure of a Belgian housewife, just as a good *kimchee* is proof of good Korean womanhood. It's an odd criterion. Basically, all you get is a plate of mini-meatballs in sauce, swimming around islands of boiled potato. It's not bad. Just plain dull.

Stoemp

Potato partially mashed together with whatever vegetable is at hand (carrots, leek, spinach, etc.). This then comes as an accompaniment to a basic protein dish (sausage, boudin, egg, or bacon). Traditionally a yokel dish, it can be found in a few restaurants as a "rediscovered" traditional dish.

Poulet Compote/Kip met appelmoes

Chicken with stewed apple. While quite acceptable eaten quietly at home, serving *poulet compote* to a middle-class Belgian guest is about as appropriate as serving pie and mash at a wedding. Some Belgian friends decided against going to a colleague's dinner party on ascertaining that their poor children were to be humiliated with *poulet compote* rather than enjoying the full adult spread.

Hutsepot

Hutsepot is a Brussels hotpot of stewed turnips, potatoes, sausages, bacon, and pigs trotters. It's supposedly traditional but I've yet to find anyone who will make it for me. Thankfully.

STREET FOOD

Offering the worst in nutrition per calorie, there are several typically local street snacks including the celebrated Belgian waffle and the mighty *frites* (chips), which really deserve a chapter of their own.

Beignet/Smoutebollen

Beignets/*Smoutebollen* are greasy fried dough balls served by the dozen in a tray of icing sugar. Playing a social role similar to candy floss, you'll only see them at the fairground. The first couple taste great: messy little treats that add to the atmosphere of roundabouts, dodgems, and teenage snogs. But by your twelfth beignet, you'll promise yourself you'll never buy them again. Until the next time.

Bilingual Belgian waffles: Gaufres or Wafels. They taste best when they are served straight from the griddle.

Caricoles

These are boiled sea snails, sold by street vendors at markets and fairs.

Gaufres/Wafels

Belgian waffles are sold hot from *patisserie* window, ubiquitous griddles in shopping centers and trolleys at special events. There's even a booth in Brussels Airport. They are served with a sprinkling of icing sugar or, more creatively, with a range of fruit, syrup, ice cream, or chocolate toppings.

Frites/Chips

French fries? Belgian fries would be much more appropriate. The Belgians take their chips very seriously. Admitting that she often feels sick after a cone of *fritches*, my wife still declares Belgian chips the best in the world. She puts it down to technique. The fries are re-fried to order so they're always fresh. The chips are also cut thin enough to get crispy but thick enough to retain the taste of potato. The partly satirical French-language Belgian website http://www.frites.be/ is full of fun, much of which is chip-related.

How Do You Spell "Chips"?

Fritches is the somewhat comic Bruxelloise term. In written Flemish, they would correctly be spelt *frieten* but are commonly rendered *fritten*. A *frituur* is the Flemish term for a chip stand, correctly written *friterie* in French but sometimes spelt as the hybrid *friture*.

Sauces for Your Chips

Any self-respecting *friture* will offer a bewildering variety of sauces to be squirted liberally on a cone of freshly fried chips. They'll charge you around 15BEF a glob for the privilege. This introduces a whole list of necessary vocabulary to ensure that your snack is not rendered inedible. As well as ketchup, mayonnaise, curry, and mustard, a typical list might include *andalouse* (like a slightly spicy Thousand Island dressing), *samurai* (similar but much spicier), *mammouth/ mammoet* (smooth and creamy), *tomagrec* (half way between ketchup and tomato purée), and *brazil* (with an intriguing fruity tang).

Chip shacks also offer a selection of unhealthy deep-fried snacks. Common examples include the pallid, lightly battered *fricandel* sausage or the *brochette tzigane* (literally gypsy kebab) which is a stick of mincemeat balls coated in spicy breadcrumbs.

REGIONAL SPECIALITIES

Areas or towns of Belgium associate themselves with gastronomic regional specialities, local produce, or a traditional local tastes. Some like *waterzooï* are now relatively widespread, but others like Poperinge's hop shoots, remain very localized and seasonal.

Antwerp	mini-cakes in the shape of a hand; *elixir d'anvers* (the local fire water); eels in green" (i.e. cooked with sorrel)
Ardennes	game (wild boar, pheasant, quail); trout; ham; a selection of cold cuts known in local dialect as *une dressée*
Arlon	*bretzel, maitrank*
Asse	*couques d'Asse*
Brakel	*geutelingen*; *mattetaarten*
Bruges	*noeuds de Bruges*
Brussels	mussels; *stoemp*; *hutspoet*

Crupet	trout
Damme	river eels
Dinant	*couques de Dinant*
Gent	*waterzooï op gentse wijze* (*à la Gantoise*); *mokken* cakes in syrup
Grammont	macaroons
Hasselt	pea soup; *jenever*; *speculoos*
Herve	smelly cheese; apple syrup
Huy	*boulettes de Huy*
Ieper	*babelutte*
Kortrijk	*kalletaart* (a long bar of pastry)
Jodoigne	cheese cake (*la blanke dorèye*)
Liège	salad *liégeoise* containing bacon, potatoes, onions, parsley, and french beans with a lukewarm vinegar-based dressing
Maaseik	*knapkoek* cake
Namur	*la flamiche* (hot, salty cheese pie); *avisances* (a sort of sausage roll); *schubertine* (trout in cream)

Nivelles	*tarte al djote* (hot flan with spicy cheese and spinach beet)
Orp-le-Petit/ Jodoigne	*boudin vert*
Poperinge	hop shoots in a cream sauce, served with a poached egg. "Popering Pears" were occasionally referred to in medieval literature (e.g. by Mercutio in Shakespeare's *Romeo and Juliet*).
Spa	mineral water; biscuits
Tongeren	*Tongerse moppen*; *caesaarkes*
Tubize	*mirandaise* tarts (sugar and almonds), adopted in 1966
Veurne	*Vernse slaper* (pastry)
Villers-la-Ville	*bâton de St Bernard* (sausage)
Virton/Arlon	*geheck*
Wavre	*tarte au stofé*
Wepion	strawberries

DINING IN BELGIUM

Entertaining

There are some basic rules to entertaining in Belgium. As anywhere, it's polite for a guest to bring a gift for the host. Flowers are generally more appropriate than wine, especially for a hostess. A 800BEF bunch should do the job: don't expect to get away with a seasonal bundle of wild daffodils sold by one of the Romanian roadside gypsies. If you bring chocolates, remember that the brand is important.

Dining on the Petite Rue des Bouchers: atmospheric and cheap if you keep your wits about you.

If you are hosting a dinner party, you'll need a well-stocked drinks cabinet as the boozing typically continues a good while before and after the meal. The aperitif drink (e.g. port, whiskey & Coke, sparkling wine) is typically served with *zakouski* snacks. The meal passes much as in any country, but remember to have chilled mineral water handy. Or, should you dare to serve tap water, hide your deceit in a misleadingly labelled mineral water bottle.

Restaurants and Chef-Artistes

Dining out in Belgium is a great pleasure. The standards are almost invariably high, and while prices are not cheap, they usually reflect a very good value for money. Set lunches and fixed *menu du jour/ dagmenu* may be even better value. The biggest problem can be too much choice. An invaluable aid for anyone eating out in Brussels and the suburbs is the annual *Delta*, a guide with an exhaustive list of eateries reviewed under various criteria such as price and cuisine style. On the web, check http://www.resto.be.

The best restaurant in the country, is widely accepted to be Comme Chez Soi. Such a unanimous acceptance of superiority seems odd, but the fact remains that you'll need to book weeks (or even months) ahead for dinner in this family-run place on the otherwise unfashionable Place Rouppe. Its chef, Pierre Wynants has been described as a "National Treasure." Other great celebrity chefs include Geert Van Hecke at De Karmeliet, Jean-Pierre Bruneau at Bruneau, Alain Deluc at the Barbizon (also Brussels), Christian Ulweling at the Moulin Hideux (Bouillon), and Christian Denis at the Clos St Denis (Tongeren).

International Cuisine

Only the bigger cities are likely to have sushi bars or Mexican fare. Indian food is a relatively exotic experience in Belgium and commensurately expensive, on par with eating Thai. Chinese food is available in almost every town, with a wide range of prices and standards.

143

Serving the sizeable North African community are plenty of couscous places and quaint cross-cultural hybrids like the Egyptian Pizzeria in Aalter, which serves pizzas baked on tandoori nan bread. Greek and Turkish restaurants are also ubiquitous.

Dining Caveats in Central Brussels

In central Brussels, the Rue des Bouchers and Petite Rue des Bouchers are narrow streets crammed with terrace restaurants. Even in winter, the open-air terraces are heaving with tourist diners and kept warm with powerful space heaters. Some of the restaurants along the streets (such as Aux Armes de Bruxelles which does an excellent *waterzooï*) are very well renowned, if pricey. But in many of the others, you should be wary before you make your order. You'll often see unbelievably reasonable prices on advertised set meals (maybe 495BEF for a three-course fish meal). These are genuine bargains, but don't be fooled. Pretty much anything else on the menu is likely to be much more expensive. When you get inside you may find that the menu list you're handed omits that "495BEF Special." Ask for it specifically if that's what you want, but remain cautious of the waiters' suggestions. Don't assume that dishes he proceeds to recommended are part of the menu deal, even if that sounds implied. Check! Usually they're not, and the tempting seafood platter which you merrily agree to is likely to cost around 2500BEF.

Also, be sure to look at the wine or drinks list and check carefully before casually ordering a bottle of *vin du patron*. While in restaurants almost anywhere else in Belgium, you'd expect such house wine to be between 400 and 800BEF/bottle (according to the class of the establishment), on these two streets, some restaurants use that Parisian trick of calling a vastly expensive fine wine as "the house special." Whoops, another 3000BEF. Don't let these slick tricks deter you from dining out elsewhere; you will be pleased to know that such practices are pretty much unheard of anywhere beyond the tiny tourist enclave mentioned.

Bistros, Cafés, and Fast Food

It's generally cheaper to eat in a bistro or café than in a full blown restaurant, though choice may be limited. Indeed, as the latter concentrates predominantly on drinks (and many don't serve food at all). Cafés are discussed in the following chapter. In fast-food terms, McDonalds' main rival is the Quick burger chain which recently took to advertising its "long burger for the long generation" in heavily accented English. As in Britain, *döner* kebabs (or pita sandwiches) constitute typical post-pub snacks. The finest *döner* I've ever tasted, ever, came from Ilhan, an unassuming Kurdish takeaway at the top end of Wolstraat in Tienen.

THE LAND OF BEER

Alcoholic drinks are every bit as important as food to the Belgian palate. Beer is the undoubted king of local beverages, but there are plenty of other distinctive drinks. For those who want to stay sober, there's always mineral water from the town which gave us the English term *spa*.

BEER

Belgium produces what many connoisseurs consider to be the world's finest beers. Beer became especially popular once the preservative effects of hops became known in the early Middle Ages. By the 16th century, visitors to the Low Countries were reportedly appalled by the huge national beer consumption. Although the 20th century has seen the number of breweries plummet from 3000 in 1900 to barely 100 at the start of the new millennium, Belgium still produces nearly 1000 different brews.

Types of Beer

The sheer variety is overwhelming. Beers can be variously divided into a selection of different style types according to brewing method (*geuze, lambic,* etc.), color (*blond(e)* is straw color, *bruin/brune* is dark), filtration (white beers are unfiltered), reputation (Trappist beers, abbey brews), etc. In addition there are a variety of systems for hinting at a beer's alcoholic strength:

- By an archaic specific-density number (For example, Rochefort 6, 8, and 10 —this is not the amount of alcohol by volume: a Rochefort 10 is actually nearer 11.5%!). The measurement of alcohol by volume is abbreviated as abv.

- By label color (e.g. Chimay—the 7% red being much more quaffable than the meaty 9% blue or darker, bitter white).

- By appellation—a *dubbel*/double is generally around 6–7% while a *trippel*/triple kicks you with a fearsome 8–10% punch.

- By the coverall hierarchy of four broad legal categories: 1–2% abv (Category III) for table beers, 3–4% (Category II) the rare *triple* table beers, 5% for standard beers including most draft lagers (Category I) and 6%+ (Category S) covering virtually the whole range of specialist ales for which Belgium is so justifiably famous.

Lager/Pilsener

The day-to-day beer for the majority of Belgians is a basic blonde lager: you can drink plenty without getting unduly plastered. Stella Artois was marketed to the top end U.K. lager market under the slogan "Reassuringly Expensive". Yet in Belgium it is quite unexotically standard: one of the "generic three" beers together with Jupiler and Maes. It's a 33-centiliter glass of such lagers that you'll be served if you just wander into a café and ask for a beer (*une bière/ pintje*). Lesser known brands include Cristal and Diekirch (from Luxembourg) plus there are the international standards like Kronenbourg, Heineken, Carlsberg, etc.

Speciality Beers

There is a hierarchy to Belgium's stronger speciality brews. Only six fall into the premier league, known as Trappist beers. All are associated with the Cistercian monastery or abbey which brews them: Orval, Chimay, Westmalle, Rochefort, Westveleteren, and St Benedictus (from Achel). There is also a non-Belgian Trappist beer— La Trappe, from the brewery of Koningshoeven in the Netherlands. Many bars and shops do stock the first three or four. But finding the others is like seeking the holy grail. The only place in the world you can ever be sure to find Westvletteren is the De Vrede café opposite the abbey itself (1.5 km or about a mile from Westvletteren village, between Ieper and De Dolle).

The second division brews are known as Abbey beers, but are not necessarily linked by more than a franchising agreement with the religious establishment whose name they bear. Grimbergen, and the wonderfully complex Leffe, are both increasingly widely available on draft. Many locals argue that in reality these brews are every bit as good as their Trappist brethren. As bars may stay open most of the night, there's no reason to resolve such discussions quickly. Look out also for Corsendonk, Witkap-Pater, Tongerlo, Affligem, and several others named after assorted saints (e.g. St Feuillien which can occasionally be found in jeroboam-sized bottles). Duvel, though not actually an Abbey beer per se, is considered to merit the rank by many a tippler.

Table Beer

You'll never find table beer in a bar. The inoffensive brew does have around 1.5% abv, but locals don't really consider it beer at all: it is traditionally served as a "soft drink" at family meals, especially for younger children. These days, consumption is dwindling, but supermarkets still sell it in 75 cl screw top bottles for a mere 25–40BEF. There are several varieties: *blond* (pale), *brune* (dark), and *multicéréal* (malty, brewed from a selection of grains). The best known brand is Piedboeuf.

Lambic and Gueuze

The uniquely Brabantine *lambic* is special because it has no added yeast. It simply sets to work fermenting itself. Miraculous enough to keep the nation Catholic, you might think. In fact, the divine fermentation is aided by airborne *Brettanomyces bruxellensis* microbes, which are apparently unique to Brussels and the Senne valley. A straight *lambic* is rarely served—it's simply too unpleasant. However, by blending lambics of different ages together you can get the arguably more palatable beer known as *gueuze* (pronounced something like *girls* without the letter *l*).

Flavored Beers and Fruity Lambics

There are other ways in which breweries improve upon a *lambic*. Faro is simply *lambic* sweetened with dark brown caramelized sugar. This is perceived as something of an old man's drink, although it's undergoing something of a revival of late. Then there are the fruity *lambic* beers. The most popular varieties are *framboise/frambozen* (made with crushed raspberries) and *kriek* (with cherries) although peach and other novelty varieties are sometimes available. The most commonly found brands are Belle-Vue and Mort Subite, but to my taste, the Timmermans and Boon brews are tarter and fresher. A flute of *framboise* may be delicious, but note that fruit beers are thought of as women's drinks. A *kriek* would not be the ideal thing to order after a rugby match when you're out with the lads.

White Beers (Witbier/Bière Blanche)

These unfiltered wheat beers are delicately flavored with orange peel and spices such as coriander. Unfiltered and thus cloudy, the tart, slightly cloying flavor is something of an acquired taste, improved with a squeeze of lemon, according to connoisseurs. Perhaps the most respected *witbier* is Hoegaarden, found on tap in bars across the country and beyond.

Other Beer Types

Several beers don't fall conveniently into any of the above style categories. Wood-aged Rodenbach is labelled *red beer* by some writers. Brews like De Koninck, Palm, and Horse Ale fall somewhere between lager and the speciality beers. There are a number of supposedly British-style ales brewed for Belgian tastes: notably John Martin's Pale Ale and Gordon's Highland Scotch which is served in a distinctive thistle-like glass. Guinness produces a special 8% abv version specifically for the Belgian market.

Beer Names

Stronger beers frequently adopt names linked to occultism, sin, and peril, presumably as a marketing gimmick. As well as the extremely popular Duvel (Devil) you'll find Satan, Lucifer, Diablos, Verboten Vruct (Forbidden Fruit), Guillotine, Brigand, Mort Subite (Sudden Death), and Delirium.

Many more names are unintentionally amusing in English: Silly beers from Silly, Prik Pils (from Oudenaarde), Slag lager (from Ninove), La Plope (from Wareme), Pee Klak (from Zottegem), and Witte Dikke (from Neerpelt).

Buying Beer

Any supermarket worth its car park offers the regular spectacle of housewives lugging home returnable 24-bottle crates of Stella, Jupiler, and Maes. The supermarkets also stock a limited range of speciality beers. Shopkeepers are increasingly aware that beers make good tourist souvenirs, so from Bruges to Bouillon you'll find an increasing choice of specialist beer shops. You can taste as well as buy at the Brasserie Delépine in whose cellars many companies leave their beers to age. You can also buy beer on-line; at http://www.beermania.be will deliver the brew of your choice.

Beer Etiquette

In a Belgian bar, there are none of the juvenile jokes linking half pints and limp wrists. That's because in all but the odd Irish pub, beers are inevitably served in sculpted 33 cl glasses which simply aren't full pints. Tap beers are given a sizeable head which is combed lovingly by the bartender. The inch of froth is considered integral to the presentation and is not a bar's ploy to save a few millilitres of brew, as some tight-fisted Brits are tempted to suspect. It is also good Belgian practice to dunk a lager glass in a sink of water before serving a *pintje*: a wet beer mug does not imply the sloppy lack of a tea towel. Where you can get shirty with your barman, however, is if your beer should come—heaven forbid—in the wrong glass. Mistakes are very unusual (except for basic lagers), and would be easily spotted as the name of the brew is prominently engraved or printed on each glass and the design for each brand has a distinctive shape.

Kwak

A unique etiquette applies to drinking Kwak from its peculiar test-tube of a glass. Its bottom is so rounded that it simply can't stand up; it's held in the precariously loose grip of a wooden stand. The drinker is expected to balance the assemblage and get the glass to his/her lips by holding the wooden rod and not the glass itself. Any jerky

Drinking Kwak is a whole new experience in itself—the unique brew has its own its glass and stand. Bottoms up? Only at your own peril.

movement could dislodge the glass and the manoeuvre becomes increasingly precarious the more one drinks. Understandably, this results in some bars demanding a deposit for their Kwak glass to ensure that breakages are paid for. In some cases, bars will take anything as a deposit—even your right shoe! Lots of fun, but be aware that locals assume most Kwak drinkers are tourists.

Some Belgian Beer Trivia

- There are beer museums in Brussels' Grand Place, at 20 Brouwerstraat Antwerp, and in the Leuven Stadhuis plus several others.

- Several working breweries are open by appointment. Straffe Hendrick in Bruges with its canal-side provides tours for "drop-in" tourists.

- Certain Belgian recipes include beer as an ingredient, most famously *carbonnades flamandes*—a beef-and-beer casserole.

- The Den Dijver in Bruges is a high-class restaurant with a gourmet menu which consists entirely of delicacies cooked with beer, each course accompanied by the appropriate brew.

- Belgians drink an annual average of 101 liters of beer per capita, making them the world's sixth largest consumers after the Germans (131 l), Irish, Danish, Austrians, and Brits (who drink a mere 2 l more).

- Around 3500 of Belgium's 27,500 bars have plaques to show that the staff have passed beer pouring exams.

- The patron saint of Belgian brewers is St Arnou, an 11th century Flemish monk who saved believers from the plague by persuading them to drink beer instead of water.

- The Bruxellois term *flotchesbeer* is a slang term for a disappointingly weak beer. A very rare problem.

WINE

Despite all the beer drinking, Belgians also consume vast quantities of wine. There are Belgian wineries but production is limited and fairly expensive so the majority of wine is imported, predominantly from France.

Belgian Wine

In the 13th century, almost every village in the Hageland region of Belgium had a vineyard on its south-facing slopes. However, in the 1430s, the Burgundian dynasty took over the region. Their taste leant toward the finer wines of France and the Rheinland, and the lower-quality Belgian industry couldn't compete. Meanwhile the introduction of hops meant that beers could keep better and were thus ever more popular amongst the poorer folk. The Hageland wine industry simply fizzled out. It was tentatively revived between 1815 and 1865 in the village of Wezemaal, protected from the vicious north winds by a unique man-made wine-wall which still stands today. The revival didn't last and the region turned to other fruits besides grapes: peaches and Jonagold apples. A second renaissance began in 1970s, and the region's vineyards have now been partially replanted.

Belgium has other wine areas in the provinces of Hainaut and Luxembourg. The Riesling-style Clos de la Zolette from the Gaume district is highly appreciated but hard to find beyond that region. Overijse on the Brussels outskirts is famous for its greenhouse-grown grapes and holds an annual Grapes in History pageant.

Imported Wine

Choosing wine poses a classic conundrum for the contradictions in the Belgian soul. On the one hand, there is the ever-present urge to seek out a bargain. On the other lurks a strong streak of French style château-snobbery in choosing which wines are "acceptable." Some Belgians consider serving a *vin de pays* (rather than a true AOC wine) akin to offering baked beans at a dinner party (See Glossary). A similar snobbism frowns on wines from "lesser regions." Even though regions like Minervois and Corbières may now be much better than their traditional reputations, God forbid that anyone should catch you uncorking a bottle in company. Of course, foreigners are suspected of wholesale ignorance. Making a bad wine choice allows everyone else to snigger behind their hands and later exclaim how uncultured the rest of the world is. The attitude is at its most

unbearable when you take a Belgian to a restaurant in Britain or the States to hear that feigned amazement: "Why is it that people here actually seem to like *vin de table*?"

Getting it Cheaper

The trouble for wine drinkers is that the stuff costs up to twice as much in Belgium as in France. Problem? Of course not. You'll find the Belgians arriving en masse at Lille or Valenciennes (just off the Brussels–Paris road). Signs within the gigantic car park of the Auchan hypermarket point its customers helpfully back to Belgium.

On one of my first visits to Belgium I was served a very good, if young wine from an unlabeled bottle. I complemented my hosts on making such an amazing home brew—my Boots DIY wine kits had never turned out anything like that. Suitably insulted, they explained that the wine was actually a very fine Bordeaux. They'd simply bottled themselves. Whoops. Bottling your own wine is another distinctly Belgian way to get cheaper wine. One family orders a big bulk shipment from a French winery. They take orders from friends and family who come round on a prescribed day for a bottling party. Everyone brings their own bottles (so save and wash your empties) and a jolly party ensues as everyone takes turns filling bottles and corking them with a special (and rather expensive) machine. A lot of wine fails to reach the bottles at all!

Port/Porto

While they don't make the stuff, Belgians are amongst the world's largest per capita consumers of port (which they quite correctly call *Porto*). *Porto* is drunk as an aperitif rather than an after-dinner snifter. And, contrary to their normal passion for quality comestibles, for some reason Belgians seem satisfied with some of the shoddiest *Portos* around. The drink is seen as cheap, and is thus destined to remain so.

OTHER BELGIAN TIPPLES

Apéritif Maison

An *apéritif maison* is not a starter course, but a restaurant's home-blended pre-prandial cocktail. This frequently combines a little white wine with a bizarre and colorful range of fruity flavors.

Jenever/Genièvre/Witteke

The town of Hasselt is famed for two liquid delicacies: pea soup and gin. Dutch-style gin, that is, known in Flemish as *jenever* and once a mainstay of local hangovers. The drink is now much less popular in Belgium than it is in Holland (where it's spelt *genever*) thanks to a century of prohibition in the 1880s which forbade Belgian cafés from serving the stuff. Only four Belgian distilleries survived the prohibition. The fact that any did at all is thanks to Flemish *jenever*'s reputation as the best available. These days attitudes have changed. Some 70 distilleries now produce over 200 varieties and there's even a National Gin Museum where you can taste dozens of *jenevers*. Just as with Belgian beers, the producers offer a great range of fruit-flavored versions. But unlike many other types of gin, *jenever* should be drunk straight, not used in cocktails.

Hasselt's version of the Manneken-Pis is the Borrelmanneke fountain. The little chap holds a *jenever* barrel with a small hole in the bottom from which the water flows. During the annual Jenever Festival, it flows with gin instead.

Péket/Péquet

This is a uniquely Belgian variant of *jenever* flavored with juniper but slightly weaker than gin. It features heavily in the September Fêtes de Wallonie in Namur with revellers pouring saké-style cupfuls for each other like raucous Japanese at *hanami*. Cups are chained to wrists for safekeeping lest they get mislaid in the drinkers' drunken stupor.

157

Elixir d'Anvers

This is a slightly sugared firewater from Antwerp.

Maitrank

This typical May Drink of the Arlon region (Luxembourg Province) is made from very dry white wine in which woodruff (*Asperula odorantis*) has been left to soak. *Maitrank* should be served very cold with a slice of orange and can be used in certain recipes for cooking mussels.

SOFT DRINKS

Belgians aren't entirely alcoholic. They consume essentially the same familiar range of nonalcoholic beverages as other Europeans. Coffee is a typical beverage at the breakfast table and after meals. Fizzy soft drinks have largely replaced table beers as the standard drink that goes with family meals.

WATER

A Belgian restaurant will happily bring you free bread with a meal. But ask for water and you'll get an expensive bottle of *eau minérale*. Beer would usually be cheaper. Although it is theoretically your right to demand tap water, no self-respecting Belgian seems capable of overcoming the stigma that ordering *eau du robinet/kraantjeswater* confers.

There are dozens of brands of mineral water named for their spring sources. High-profile Belgian examples are Chaudfontaine and Spa. The latter has been associated with curative water treatments for so long that its name and associated function have been adopted into the English language.

BARS AND CAFÉS

In Belgium the term *café* can denote a vast range of possible establishments but all are more likely to be what English speakers would define as a pub or bar. Unlike French bars and cafés, relatively few Belgian cafés serve food . You might get cubes of cheese, slices of salami, or nuts from a dispenser or maybe, if you are lucky, a sandwich or *croque monsieur*. Spaghetti or light meals are offered by certain cafés with a sign in the window saying "*Petite Restauration.*"

Some cafés are fabulous architectural gems but many more are dismal, barely decorated brick boxes where sorry-looking regulars say their hellos and then settle to a smoky night (or day) of solitary swigging. Belgium has an astonishing number of cafés: one for every 407 people. The rather dismal town of Mouscron, otherwise famed only for the occasional success of its football team, has a café for every 218 inhabitants.

A bar, to the Belgians, is a more upscale place. A cocktail den like Ricks on Brussels' Avenue Louise, perhaps. Or the bar of a hotel: anywhere that the drinks wear bow ties. Somewhere in between bars and cafés are the city pubs, often aimed at the expatriate crowd.

Café Types
Broadly speaking there are three main types of cafés. I've dubbed these "charmers," "squealers," and "locals." Like the three primary colors, one can observe every shade of overlap between them.

Venerable Charmers
The most obviously attractive bars are the wonderful Art Nouveau, turn-of-the-century places; all polished brass, old mirrors, and carved wood. Greatest amongst these are the Falstaff, the Cirio, and the Mort Subite, all in Brussels. But most of the bigger towns have an equivalent, and in the countryside, several beer brewing abbeys have a pub nearby or *en site* so that you can sample the brew. Not all charmers are old. Some are simply well situated with a nice summer terrace. The only possible down side of these places is that for all their atmosphere, you'll rarely find yourself thrust into bizarre conversations with the locals. Reckon on 60–80BEF for a *pintje*.

159

Young Squealers

The teenager crowd tends to migrate toward the modern décor and loud music of cafés that look like bars almost anywhere in the Western Hemisphere. They have relatively dim lighting and a remarkable preponderance of people who seem blissfully oblivious to all the Smoking Causes Cancer campaigns. Prices similar: 50–80 for a *pintje* as long as you stick to non-imported beer.

Unpretentious Locals

These most archetypal Belgian bars are outwardly depressing dives. Typically, they're shoebox-shaped shop units marked with plain Maes, Stella, or Jupiler name signs. The sheer lack of adornment can at times be astonishing. Inside, you'll find tables to one side, a row of stools to the other, and a bored bartender making strained banter with a motley selection of old, predominantly male, social misfits. These places are an anthropologist's dream. The price for a *pintje* is low— around 45 to 50BEF. A photographer specializing in strawberry noses and bizarre facial hair could find the opportunities overwhelming. Even a fellow Belgian may occasionally require an interpreter.

Don't venture in if you want a quiet drink: once you've overcome the "all eyes on the stranger" entry, half the locals may decide to nestle in for a chat. It's a real opportunity for cultural immersion.

Country Pubs

The quaint country pubs familiar across the U.K. are relatively rare in Belgium. There are certainly café-pubs in villages, but they are typically very much of the brick-box local variety: often sadly unappealing. However, there are some notable exceptions. Examples around Brussels include two renovated watermills near Grimbergen, of which the Tommonmolen is the most atmospheric. There is a peaceful lakeside terrace at Sept Fontaines' La Piñeta, (off the Chaussée d'Alsemberg, south of Sint-Genesius-Rode) though this is frequently reserved for diners. You'll have to pay the 120BEF entry to the stately Great Park to reach Enghien/Endigen's delightful little Halte du Miroir. A personal favorite is the sunset terrace beside the moat of Horst Castle, 7 km (4.2 miles) south of Aarschot down a quiet country lane from St Pieters-Rode. For homely stalwart village inns where you can expect to be served by waddling old dears in black dresses with white aprons, and incomprehensible jokes, there's a classic in Villers-la-Ville or try the Huis Istas in Jezus-Eik, just beyond the Brussels Ring.

Bars Without a "Key"

The notorious 24-hour bars are not as common as some would have you believe. Still, wandering around Brussels cafés between 5 and 8 a.m. one Saturday (for research purposes only, you understand), I found an ample selection of watering holes still more than happy to pour me a *pintje*. And without cover charges or excessively inflated prices either.

Beer Cafés

This sounds like a contradiction in terms as all bars and cafés have beers by the dozen. A beer café, however, is one where the choice of brews is so long you need a multi-paged menu to list them all. These are more common than you might imagine. Classics include Brussels' Moeder Lambic, Antwerp's Kulminator, and the Rembrandt on Enghien's Grand Place.

Bar Games

Cafés aimed at the younger market often have video games, table football, pinball machines, or perhaps a pool table. Others encourage old men to play dominoes or cards. And the Greenwich, a delightfully unpretentious Art Nouveau café in central Brussels, is the place to play chess. Once you get there, you'll notice that pretty much every table is likely to be deep in concentration over a game. There is no charge for the use of the sets and it's often possible to find other people to play against should you happen to walk in alone.

Why fly to Las Vegas (or drive to Ostend) if your local café has Den Tosh?

Traditional cafés also have a couple of distinctly Belgian games including a version of "American" billiards in which two holes are positioned well away from the cushions and guarded by rubber mushrooms.

More common is Den Tosh, a wonderfully archaic looking machine halfway between pinball and a fairground game. The aim is to get a series of balls to lodge in a specified set of numbered holes. Like in Japanese *pachinko*, there are no flippers, so there is little you can do to affect where the ball ends up. However, by feeding in more money you can rearrange "win grids" and buy extra balls to improve your chances. On the face of it, all this is purely for fun. Gambling is not allowed in cafés (one-arm bandit slot machines are relegated to gaming rooms and casinos) so in Den Tosh you simply win "credits" to play again. Cafés often tacitly agree to "buy back" any credits won, however, thereby encouraging gamblers to play for stakes vastly higher than the paltry 5BEF minimum.

General Etiquette for Belgian Cafés and Bars

- Except, perhaps, in a few expatriate bars, tipping the bar staff is utterly unnecessary.

- Drinks will be brought to your table unless noted otherwise. *"Bestellen aan de bar a.u.b./ commander au bar s.v.p."* means "please order at the bar."

- Rather than charge for each successive round of drinks, most cafés run a tab that you pay just before leaving.

- Better bars often provide a little thimble full of peanuts or mini-crackers to accompany your drink. This doesn't cost extra, and in some places there's a large bowl from which you can freely replenish your supply. In cheaper places you may have to put a 20BEF coin into a snack dispenser. Some cafés also have a basic snack, sandwich, and meal menu and virtually all serve decent coffee.

- In neighboring Holland, it is normal behavior to hang up your coat at the entry to a café or bar. This habit is not generally practised by less trusting Belgium drinkers, who feel safer draping their coats over their chairs where they can keep an eye on them.

Chapter Eleven

BUSINESS AND WORK

Belgian attitudes to work are something of a paradox. The country is in many ways delightfully uncommercial with a noticeable socialist lean to most governmental policy. Yet in their souls, Belgians are money-minded. The taunt "He's no *comerçant*" was the worst thing you could say about a person in West Flanders, according to the hero's Grandpa in *The Sorrow of Belgium*. Whether to save a penny on the house-keeping, to cheat the tax man, or simply to devise a money-making plan, most Belgians will rise to the challenge. When work interferes with eating a hearty dinner, however, or offers only a marginal profit, then interest wanes very quickly. Well, why not let the Turkish or Moroccan fellow run the corner shop if he really wants to stay open after 6:30 p.m.?

Belgian employers generally offer relatively generous staff benefits and the average working week is short. Many bigger firms appear relatively inefficient but are still better than bureaucratic government organizations from which ordinary citizens have very low expectations of any kind of service.

PAY

"Positions vacant" notices in the Belgian press rarely state the salary available. You'll have to check. Like most Westerners, Belgians are not keen to disclose their income in conversation. But even if they do, they are likely to quote a monthly sum rather than an annual one. This is misleading because no full-time Belgian employee receives as little as 12 months' pay. Companies must give an extra 85% of one month's salary as "holiday pay," typically in early summer. Then at the end of December, most companies give another extra month's bonus—generous companies give two! Add to all this the luncheon vouchers, company health insurance top-ups, and the relatively frequent award of a company car for people in middle management positions: no wonder the Belgians don't seem to be doing badly.

On the down side, taxes are pretty heavy. My wife has a relatively modest salary by local standards, but pays more than 50% in taxes, social security, and other assorted contributions. Tax cuts are promised in 2001, but are unlikely to be significant.

WORKING "IN BLACK"

Anything that is "in black" involves an element of tax avoidance. And in Belgium, the majority of the population see tax evasion as a lighthearted national sport rather than a crime. This applies particularly to the self employed who are subject to a particularly withering fiscal barrage. By doing undeclared work, they can easily double their incomes. Customers and self-employed workmen (electricians, plumbers, etc.) are frequently in cahoots: "I don't need a receipt if you don't charge me VAT". A voucher scheme introduced in 1999 allowed you to purchase cheap credits toward various home improvement work at knockdown prices, assuming that you used reputable, taxpaying workmen who could cash the vouchers and who would declare the work to the authorities. Predictably, this proved very expensive and was rapidly scrapped.

CORRUPTION

One friend joked: "We like to think of ourselves as the small, sick boy of Europe. We're not as corrupt as Italy, but if we try a little harder we could be!" In 1988, a payment of over $1,700,000 from the Italian aircraft manufacturer Agusta made its way to the accounts of the governing socialist party. Hey presto, the Belgian Army proceeded to purchase over 40 Agusta helicopters.

The 1990s also saw some pretty high-level scandals. Around a dozen ministers of the national government were sacked in various corruption cases. Most famously, Willy Claes (who had been Minister of Economics at the time) was finally pressured into resigning in 1995—a particularly newsworthy event as he had by that stage risen to the post of NATO Secretary General. Claes received a three-year suspended sentence.

Belgium is trying to shed its reputation as the most corrupt nation in northern Europe. However, the coalition-style government structure doesn't make radical reform at all easy. Since most of the upper bureaucracy is appointed according to political favor, a call from an MP can get rules bent, planning permission pushed through, or jobs found for a nagging citizen in return for their votes and those of their grateful family. Certainly MPs all over the world meet and listen to their constituents' needs and concerns. But the Belgian MPs' *zitdag* surgeries, or parliamentary surgeries, are, according to one local journalist, little more than deals for votes.

BUREAUCRACY

There's a thick layer of bureaucracy. And because of the multiple divisions in society between linguistic groups, communal and regional interests, and political factions, much gets duplicated.

In government jobs, there has traditionally been a high level of political interference. Again, there have been reforms, but until recently in most higher government positions, promotion relied upon your political affiliations. Ironically, that did not always mean that you were wise to join the biggest party of the ruling coalition. With postings shared amongst those with affiliations to each ruling partner, the ideal was to find who of the potential candidates were in which parties and join the one which seemed the least represented. Given the reforms, job promotion nowadays depends mainly on merit, but there is still a suspicion that for the highest posts, language balance and political affiliation remain important factors.

UNEMPLOYMENT

The unemployed are paid a fairly generous allowance but, unlike in the U.K., rent is not covered by the local council. Benefits are often paid indirectly through the unemployed person's trade union, and an annual "holiday" is allowed during which time one doesn't have to show up to sign.

A surprising number of unemployed people are employed "in black," or illegally, by businesses who thereby avoid a slew of social security obligations and can pay a lower salary to the employed "unemployed" than to others who don't have the dole as an extra income. Attitudes toward this sort of activity seem to be surprisingly tolerant, except perhaps where the beneficiary is a "foreigner."

167

UNIONISM

Unions in Belgium are primarily divided by political loyalty rather than by trade. There are thus three major unions, broadly socialist, liberal, and Christian. Bigger businesses are required to have a management–union committee for which a selection of union representatives is elected to represent the workers. This applies to all sectors, not just industrial labor. However, white collar employees are generally apathetic or wary: there's a middle-class disdain for unionism and union membership is quietly acknowledged to curtail any hopes of rapid promotion. On the other hand, those who stand for representative positions are afforded a remarkable level of legal protection against redundancy if they can show that their dismissal had anything to do with their union activities. This even applies to those who stand for election but are not elected.

BELGIAN BUSINESSES

The archetypal Belgian industries are the production of chocolate and beer and construction. Although no longer the world's second industrial power, a pinnacle achieved very briefly in the late 19th century, industrial companies like Electrabel, Bekaert, Beaulieu, and Solvay remain major world players and stand to gain from the recent (March 2000) decision to merge the Brussels, Amsterdam, and Paris stock exchanges. Belgium has also marketed itself very successfully as a hub for international couriers and for financial institutions. DHL has its trans-European shipment center here. Members of the management body of SWIFT are based near Brussels and MasterCard's European operations are run by the Belgian Europay International company in Waterloo.

Antwerp has long been and remains the world center for diamond cutting and trading. See the website http://www.diamonds.be/ for more information.

CURRENCY AND MONEY

Thanks to a historical quirk in exchange rates and inflation indices, the Belgian franc was one of the world's most sensibly denominated currencies. The smallest unit you ever needed was 1BEF, although 50 centime (1/2 franc) coins did exist. Nonetheless Belgians seem unperturbed to see their once stable currency subsumed within the Euro, a process which should be well underway by the time you read this.

Belgians are as paradoxical in their attitudes to money as in their business sense. It's considered sensibly practical that advertisements appear on state radio and TV (despite a license fee) and sponsors even pay for certain communes' road signs. Many housewives and old ladies assiduously plough through the dozens of free magazines and supermarket fliers that clog up the mail, searching for bargains and coupons. Meanwhile the same individuals will have you believe that there are some stores that are just too "low-class" to be seen in.

Chapter Twelve

ENTERTAINMENT
AND THE ARTS

"Belgian art?—Do you mean lace-making or the Manneken-Pis?"
Foreigners have a grossly unfair disdain for Belgium's contributions
in the field of the arts. Not all the decorative arts are sold from kitschily
twee souvenir boutiques in Bruges. Indeed some of the greatest artists
in history came from Belgian soil.

EARLY ARTISTS

Before the 15th century, European painters had a pretty wobbly feel
for perspective and concentrated mostly on religious subjects or
portraits of noble patrons. Flemish artists were the first to really

change this. Jan van Eyck (1390–1441), one of the artists known as the Flemish Primitives, certainly started out painting royal mug shots —indeed his portrait of Isabella of Portugal was so good that his master Philip the Good decided to marry her. But along with his brother Hubert, Jan perfected oil painting, allowing previously unprecedented levels of realism.

Flemish artists started backing portraits with landscapes instead of solid colors or gold leaf. These glimpses of everyday life would eventually become subjects in themselves. This was encouraged by the new wealth of the Flemish merchants who were happy to pay enticing fees for painted "snap shots" of their families, homes, and possessions.

Other great Flemish Primitives of the same era include the artists Rogier van der Weyden (1399–1464), Hugo van der Goes (1440–1482), and Hans Memling (1435–1494, a naturalized Bruges citizen though born in Frankfurt). Great places to see their works include the Groeninge museum in Bruges and the Gallerie des Beaux Arts in Brussels. The collected works of the van Eycks are exhibited in their entirety (albeit in photographic reproduction) at the Couvent des Frères Mineurs on Boomgaardstraat in Maaseik.

In this period, tapestry-making was every bit as important as painting. Especially for the then Flemish town of Arras, it was a major craft-industry, and one which moved en masse to Brussels when artists fled in 1477, following Arras's annexation and destruction by French king Louis IX. Fine examples of medieval Belgian tapestries are displayed in the Maison du Roi on Brussels' Grand Place.

RENAISSANCE AND BAROQUE

Sixteenth century Flemish painting styles varied considerably. Contrast the Leonardo De Vinci inspired realism of artists like Quentin Metsys/Matsijs (1465–1530), with the surreal imagery of the Breughels, which belongs in the darkly bizarre pictorial world of Hieronymous Bosch. Some of the most remarkable canvases in

Brussels' Heulens Van der Mieren collection are landscapes peopled with contorted anthropomorphic figures. The names of their artists are unknown (the paintings are not signed), but were they not 450 years old, it would be tempting to suspect they were the works of Salvador Dali.

The Manneken Pis (1619): a humorously ironic choice of icon for a country of such artistic pedigree.

The aftermath of the Dutch revolts meant that art as well as the economy and culture of 17th century Belgium were force-fed heavy doses of Catholicism. The great paintings of the new era tried to ram home the message with vast, overpowering images of sumptuous heavens and brooding hells.

Despite the drastic decline in trade, Antwerp developed as a formidable artistic center thanks in part to a trio of great painters Peter Paul Rubens (1577–1640), Anthony (Antoon) Van Dyck (1599–1641) (who was later appointed court painter to Charles I of England), and Jacob Jordaens (1593–1678). The works of these and other great Baroque artists are to be found in many Belgian museums and churches. On August 15, Antwerp celebrates with a Rubens Market: stall-holders dress up in period costumes, adding to the charm of the antique market on Handschoenmarkt.

19TH AND 20TH CENTURY ART

Independent Belgium developed a range of artistic talents including the Romantic/Neoclassical Antoine Wiertz (1806–1865), great naturalist Constantin Meunier (1831–1905), and the symbolist Ferdinand Knopff (1853–1921) whose delightful work echoes the pre-Raphaelites and deserves a much wider appreciation. Belgium was one of the first places to embrace the naturalistic curves and serifs of Art Nouveau, notably in decorative arts, furniture, and architecture. Belgians are almost universally proud of the elegant buildings by architects Henri van der Velde (1863–1957), Paul Hankar (1859–1901), and especially Victor Horta (1861–1947). Yet oddly little was done to protect that heritage until relatively recently (See Chapter Five).

Remarkably ahead of his time, James Ensor, (1860–1949), was an Ostend-born pre-Expressionist painter whose works ranged from attractive Manet-like scenes to macabre masks and human faces with a dash of Van Gogh. He is particularly *en vogue* at present since a major retrospective in Brussels 1999 on the 50th anniversary of his death. Probably the greatest 20th century Belgian artist was René

173

Magritte (1898–1967). His surrealist figures are notable for their lack of faces as in *Les Amants* where a pair of lovers kiss, apparently oblivious to the bags across their heads. His most famous painting strikes a particularly resonant chord with the Belgian sense of the absurd. It is a simple depiction of a pipe. Underneath, the prominently inscribed title proclaims (in French) "This is not a pipe". See http://www.virtuo.be/ for more Magritte images.

The Belgian surrealist Paul Delvaux has gained a certain notoriety for his obsessively repetitive theme of semi-surrealist nudes, almost universally based on his wife. There's a museum of his work in Sint-Idesbald. Harry Pearson in his hilarious book *Tall Man in a Low Land* notes that Delvaux's bust in Veurne, peeps most appropriately through the bushes at a statue of a naked girl.

MODERN AND CONTEMPORARY ART

Without much fanfare, Belgium continues to drape itself in art, albeit to mixed reviews. Large, lumpy metal-&-stone hunks sometimes prove remarkably appealing, as along the Franklin Rooseveltlaan in Brussels. Other examples are downright peculiar, like the strange rusty structure outside Turnhout Station: a gigantic, bent "tuning fork" with a rock precariously balanced on its tip. Like it or loathe it, new art is everywhere, from *trompe l'oeil* murals to the intimidatingly colorful graffitti of suburban railway halts. The effect is to insert unexpected visual stimuli amid the mediocrity of even the drabbest suburbs. You may have to wait a while for the Brussels metro, but at least there's something to look at: each station has been decorated by different contemporary artists. And around the capital, the walls of 25 unsightly end-of-terrace houses have been adorned with what is arguably that most popular of all Belgian art forms: the cartoon strip.

Cartoon Strips (Bande Dessinée/Stripverhaal)

Belgians (adults just as much as children) have a passion for comic books that is second only to that of the Japanese. cartoons are taken

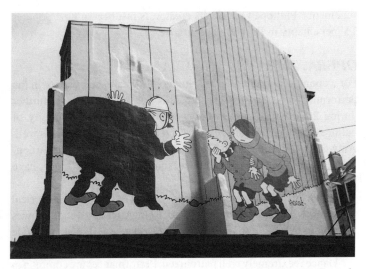

Hergé's Quick and Flupke get down to some comic peeping tommery on a Brussels end-of-terrace house wall.

seriously as an art form and most Belgian homes quietly shelter a shelf or two of hardbound albums.

Internationally, Hergé's Tintin and Peyo's Schtroumpf (Smurfs) are probably Belgium's best known *bande dessinée* characters. But dozens of others are household names locally. Many Belgians are astounded to discover that characters like the lonesome cowboy Lucky Luke are not world-famous. Other classics to read if you want to sound knowledgeable include Vandersteen's *Suske & Wiske/Bob & Bobette*, Franquin's *Gaston Lagaffe* and *Spirou*, and Hergé's *Quick & Flupke*. A visit to the Centre Belge de la Bande Dessinée comic museum will introduce you to many more.

Belgium's political cartoonists can be merciless on the country's leaders. Astute observers include Vadot in *Le Vif L'Express* and Kroll in the *Tele Moustique* magazine. Le Chat is a ubiquitous single frame cartoon character who is fond of making obvious yet sagacious

175

statements. Philippe Geluck, its creator, is fast becoming a popular TV personality in Belgium and France.

OPERA, THEATER, AND DANCE

For a country so small, there's remarkable wealth and variety in the performing arts. In Brussels, the selection improved even further during 2000 with Brussels being appointed the European city of culture. But other areas have a very lively dramatic arts scene as well. Antwerp (all summer) and Gent (nine days in late July) are particularly active during their festival seasons and both, like Liège, have their own opera houses.

While opera is not exactly mainstream, it has a curious historical importance beyond that of the music itself. After all, Belgium owes its very existence to a 1830 opera performance at La Monnaie/De Munt (See Chapter Two).

Dance is extremely well patronized. Performances are common in a variety of styles and both Flanders and Wallonia have their own Royal Ballet companies—the latter based in the unlikely setting of post-industrial Charleroi. Although it moved to Lausanne in 1988, Belgian dance fans are proud that Maurice Béjart's groundbreaking "Ballet of the 20th Century" company and Mudra dance school were based in Brussels from 1960. There are a number of dance festivals; one for international folk groups is held at the dramatic venue of the Schoten castle during the second weekend of July (tickets from 200BEF, tel 03 658 1058).

Unlike London or New York, the Brussels theater scene is not dominated by long-running slick musicals, although when these arrive for brief spells (like French smash hit *Notre Dame de Paris* in Brussels and a Flemish version of *Les Misérables* in Antwerp), they tend to sell out very fast.

Puppet theaters were once very popular and were regarded as the poor man's TV. There are still half a dozen in Gent. In Brussels, however, there's only one left: Toone (21 Petite Rue des Bouchers), with a collection of 1200 puppets.

CINEMA

The good news for Anglophone movie-goers is that you can find most English-language films screened in VO, i.e. subtitled rather than dubbed. In smaller cinemas, beware of the dreaded usherette. In return for tearing your ticket and handing you a free magazine, she expects a 20BEF tip. Refusing to pay up may cause a scene. Some places still

The Nova is Brussels' art house cinema. Despite a great "student-style" bar and an imaginatively esoteric play list, it continues to teeter at the edge of bankruptcy.

retain these uniquely Belgian dragons. But they're a dying breed since the 1990s with the opening of big U.S.-style multi-screen cinemas (notably Kinepolis and Imagibraine).

The major cities each have their own film festivals and Brussels and Antwerp film museums screen art movies, popular classics, and dust off old, rare spools for the connoisseurs. On summer weekends from July to August, the park around Brussels' Cinquantenaire transforms into one of the world's more idiosyncratic drive-in movie theaters. You get the sound on the car radio.

Belgian Films and Film Stars

"Muscles from Brussels" Jean Claude Van Damme was born Jean Claude van Varenburg. In 1999 he deigned to come home to Belgium for his wedding—his fifth marriage. To action film aficionados, he's the greatest star on the planet. But for some Belgians, the upstart 5'8" fist-fighter is only marginally more appealing as a national symbol than chips and child molesters. It's easier to be proud of the timeless screen idol Audrey Hepburn who was also born in Brussels (as Edda Kathleen van Heemstra Hepburn-Ruston). Star of *My Fair Lady* and *Breakfast at Tiffany's* her first known screen role was a non-credited bit part in a 1948 teach-yourself Dutch/Flemish instruction film! Understandably *Nederlands in Zeven Lesen* was not a great box office storm. Indeed, until recently, the world seemed blissfully unaware of the Belgian movie industry. OK, so even today it's not Hollywood, or even Shepperton. But Belgian films have been claiming great critical success in the last few years, thanks to Chantal Akerman's *La Captive* (inspired by Proust's *La Prisonnière*) and Luc and Jean-Pierre Dardenne's *Rosetta*.

Presenting the harrowing, harsh life of a no-hope, fired factory hand, *Rosetta* is a brilliant close-up view of life in a dismal Liège backwater and was the first Belgian movie to take the Cannes Palme d'Or (1999). It also won best actress award for Emilie Dequenne, a remarkable teenage actress in the lead role. Another Belgian success was Mike van Diem's *Karakter* which won the 1998 Foreign Film Oscar. It featured Jan Decleir who also played in the 1992 Oscar-nominated *Daens*, directed by fellow Belgian Stijn Coninx. The most popular Belgian movies amongst local cinema-goers were probably *Ma Vie en Rose*, about a boy growing up wanting to be a girl, and *Le Huitième Jour*, Jaco van Dormael's moving tale of a Down's syndrome sufferer. Van Dormael's *Toto le Héros* and *Between Heaven and Earth* also received critical acclaim.

Other Belgian directors to watch out for include Jan Bucquoy (*The Sexual Life of the Belgians*, 1994; *Camping Cosmos*, 1996), André

Delvaux (*L'homme au Crâne Rasé*, 1965; *Un Soir, Un Train*, 1968), Jean-Paul Picha (*The Big Bang*, 1987), and Benoît Poelvoorde (director/actor) whose *Man Bites Dog* (1992 with Rémy Belvaux and André Bonzel) was a disturbing classic—like *Natural Born Killers* set in Namur.

What's it like to be a Belgian Movie Star?

Dark-eyed Belgian beauty Marie Gillain, was the star of *Le Dernier Harem* and a model for Lancôme. She raised great local press interest in 1999 by her improbable confession, *"C'est très à la mode d'être Belge"* ("It's very trendy to be Belgian"). Wow. At last.

MUSIC

Classical

By the age of 11, Liège-born César Franck (1822–1890) was already touring the then brand new country as a piano prodigy. Even if you don't recognize the name, you'll probably recognize his "Symphony in D Minor." Other Belgian composers include André Grétry (1731–1813), Henri Vieuxtemps (1820–1881), and Paul Gilson (1865–1942). My wife claims she only knows these names because they are streets in Brussels.

These days, Philippe Boesmans is Belgium's foremost composer of contemporary opera, having created *Reigen* in 1993 and *Wintermärchen* in 1999. The latter is based loosely on Shakespeare's *A Winter's Tale*.

Arguably Belgium's most prestigious musical event is the Concours Reine Elisabeth/Koningin Elisabethwedstrijd: a contest to find the world's best young classical singers, composers, and musicians. Started in 1937 by violin impresario Eugene Ysaye (1858–1931), it soon received the patronage of Queen Elisabeth, the wife of King Albert I and Ysaye's most famous violin student. It's held in May. See http://www.concours-reine-elisabeth.be for more details.

Jazz and Blues

Not surprisingly, the country which gave the world the saxophone is passionate about jazz. In Belgium, the term is interpreted in its widest possible sense to encompass everything from avant-garde to zydeco. There is also a vein of great soukous/*zingé* music to be mined thanks to the Congolese community based around the Matongé area of Brussels. Mainstream pop-radio carries regular "Blues and Boogie" shows. There's a Liège blues festival and the Brussels Jazz Marathon (in late May) is one of the city's most festive weekends.

Internationally, perhaps the best known Belgium-born jazz star was Django Reinhardt (1910–1953), the great gypsy guitarist who joined violin maestro Stefan Grappelli in the quintet Hot Club de France. A living legend is the recently knighted Toots Thielemans, one of the world's only musicians who've managed to make a career out of playing the harmonica. Other locally renowned jazz greats include Philippe Catherine, Charles Loos, Steve Houben, and the experimental cello and bassist José Bedeur.

Popular Music

Belgian popular music is heavily divided along linguistic lines, although both communities eagerly lap up American and British rock, dance and pop music too. French French music is also a mainstay of Francophone radio play. Contemporary bands have often taken to singing in English to gain more international exposure. Throughout the summer, rock festivals are held almost weekly and many (notably Wechter and Pukkelpop) attract big names from all over the world.

French-language Belgian stars

Jacques Brel (1928–1978) is one of the classic "3 B's" that rule the pantheon of popular French music (along with Georges Brassens and Gilbert Bécaud). Yet he was Brussels-born, and evoked Belgium in some of his classic songs ("Le Plat Pays," "Les Flamandes") which ranged from heartrending ballads to bittersweet cabaret numbers. Adamo (Salvador Adamo)—now a UNICEF envoy as well as top-selling singer and songwriter—has proved one of the most successful figures in French-language pop. His 1963 classic "Tombe la Neige" has been covered by an astounding 500 other performers. Adamo was born to one of those Italian mining families who had settled in Belgium in return for a ton of coal. His career started as a child when he secretly participated in a singing contest to win himself 2 kg (4.4 lb) of chocolate. Flame-haired Axelle Red is a more recent star in Francophone countries. But despite her wistful French lyrics, she's in fact Flemish. Despite being long defunct, Dani Klein's group Vaya con Dios remains popular, having adopted Latin rhythms long before the present fad made them trendy. Other major Belgian stars include Maurane, Annie Cordy (also a comedienne and actress), and the Canada-based songstress Lara Fabian who has been labelled the "new Céline Dion" (a compliment?).

French French Pop
To socialize with Francophones it may be tactful to develop a liking (or at least tolerance) for French chanson: a catchall term for everything from melodic ballads to insipid soft-rock. Its also wise to familiarize yourself with at least some of the classic stars of French French pop. Eternal rocker Johnny Hallyday (part Belgian, born Jean Philippe Smets) is the French Elvis. Charles "For Me… Dable" Aznavour remains one of the great crooners along with the 3B's (see above). Cringe at Claude "Clo-Clo" François's videos. Mourn for Michel Berger. Wonder how alcoholic Serge Gainsbourg managed to bed Brigit Bardot or ask anyone what he said to Whitney Houston on live TV. Gainsbourg becomes more fashionable every year, even though he's been dead for a decade. Other long-standing stars include goat-voiced Julien Clerc, heartthrob Patrick Bruel, and veteran rapper MC Solar. Classic female artists include Sylvie Vartan, France Gall, and the ever-warbling Véronique Sanson.

181

The Lotti Paradox

Where middle-of-the-road chanson crosses into pop, you'll find a Belgian reigning as the unlikely king of the European ratings. Helmut Lotti, a Flemish Mr Clean singer from Gent, is the Belgian Barry Manilow and presently the top-selling artist in the Benelux. He started his career as an Elvis impersonator, and since his second album has given up singing in *Nederlands* (the language, not the country). The antithesis of a rock archetype, he usually appears neatly groomed in a smart suit and tie. He continues to be successful by singing a vast range of styles from pop to opera to African, each accompanied by soaring symphonic background and rock beat. Seen as every mother's ideal son in law, he is an embarrassing joke to many: interviewed on radio, even his biographer was swift to deny being a fan. Nonetheless there remain vast hordes of loyal Lotti followers, 90% female (see http://www.helmutlotti.be).

Flemish Folk Music

Many contemporary Flemish bands sing in English (see below). For the best selection of Flemish folk CDs, visit Den Appel in Asse. Styles range from ponderous polkas to haunting pseudo-Irish melodies, or folk music heavy on the fiddle.

Lais is the Flemish folk movement's equivalent of the Corrs: three young women producing music of striking variety from highly traditional semi-Gaelic sounds to rock-beat hoedown. They even sing occasionally in French or Swedish! Arno (Arno Hintjens) also sings in three languages. Don't confuse Lais with Lucy Loes, a rotund septuagenarian "um-pah" singer, dubbed the queen of Ostend fisherfolk ballads.

Contemporary Belgian Rock

Rockers SweateR and club stars dEUS are amongst the latest proponents of the mis-spell-your-way-to-fame approach pioneered years before by fellow Belgian group Sttellla. Along with K's Choice ("I'm not an addict", "Everything for free"), dEUS are probably the best known band to emerge from the very active 1990s Antwerp music scene. Conservatory-trained DAAU combines clarinets and strings, with samples and synths for a unique musical blend with varied influences including hip-hop and reggae. Hooverphonic, once pigeonholed as a trip-hop act are in fact a boundary-breaking band from St Niklaas who deserve the international fame toward which they appear to be edging during 2001. For more up-to-date information on the Belgian music scene, see http://houbi.com/belpop/links.htm.

Memorable One-offs

British thirty-somethings probably remember the very brief appearance of Le Punk when Belgian misfit Plastic Bertrand's catchy if monotonous ditty "Ça Plane pour Moi" became an unlikely U.K. hit. About as punk as Abba, he swiftly disappeared and his appalling attempt at a revival with a Belgian entry for the Eurovision Song Contest was an unmitigated failure. Indeed Belgium's only success in that competition was in 1986, the night before the Chernobyl disaster. The winner was a 14-year-old schoolgirl by the name of Sandra Kim (real name Sandra Caldarone) who declared herself "Italian by extraction, Walloon at heart". The greatest Eurovision failure was Fud Leclerc who represented Belgium in 1958, 1960, and 1962, and on the last occasion managed astoundingly to score no points whatever, a feat nearly repeated in 2000 by Nathalie Sorce who finally scooped a pitiful three votes. This resulted in Belgium being booted out of the May 2001 competition, a fact heralded with typical self-effacing humor in *Télé Moustique* with the quip: "Belgium—no point". The most bizarre of all Belgian one-off's was the annoyingly catchy little song that starts, "Domini-ka-nik-a-ni-que" and went on to chart success right across Europe. It was sung by Soeur Sourire (aka Janine Deckers) a gay nun who ended up committing suicide in Wavre.

TELEVISION

For obvious practical reasons, the press and entertainment industries are divided along linguistic lines. What is surprising is how rabidly independent the apparently equivalent institutions are in relation to one another. British or American programs may be dubbed or subtitled in French or Flemish but Belgian programs almost never cross the linguistic divide. Each community admits knowing more about the rest of Europe than about the other Belgium.

The main terrestrial TV networks are state-run VRT (in Flemish) and RTBF (in French) plus VTM (Flemish) and RTL (nominally from Luxembourg but focussed on Francophone Belgium).

Belgian news programs (in French at 7 p.m. on RTL and 7:30 p.m. on RTBF1; in Flemish at 7 p.m. and 11 p.m. on TV1 7 p.m. on VTM) are reassuringly down-to-earth without the infuriating breaks, pointless conjectural pontificating, or constant headline recaps of BBC, CNN, etc. Reports are laced with ironic humor rather than confrontational interviews so unlike in the U.K., and politicians are generally prepared to speak candidly off the cuff. Although RTBF and VRT are government-run and subject to political influence, they are generally seen to be fair and neutral, although TV news does tend to plug Belgian folkloric events and business deals.

You'll have to pay a license fee of around 7608BEF for a color set to the Service Redevances Bureau in Wallonia, or the equivalent in Brussels or Flanders. On top of this, you'll have to pay an extra fee if you want cable connection (2–3000BEF connection plus around 4000BEF/year subscription). Some 90% of households do have cable TV, making Belgium the most cabled country anywhere. With access to more than 30 channels virtually anyone can flick between programs in German, Spanish, and English (typically CNN, BBC1 and 2, CNBC, and MTV). Many households receive Portuguese and Turkish programming too. Ironically, the cable companies often fail to provide the full range of Flemish channels in Wallonia or Francophone Belgian channels in Flanders. For the linguistically challenged TV addict wanting a wider range of English-language programs, there is a slight advantage to living in Brussels or Flanders as many subtitled foreign programs appear only on Flemish channels (such as *Frasier* on VTM, *Jonathon Creek* on Canvas, *Friends* and *Cheers* on VT4, etc.).

If the standard cable selection doesn't offer enough choice you can add further pay channels (like Canal Plus) or get a satellite dish. Beware of possible installation restrictions on your house/apartment lease if you opt for the latter.

RADIO

As in Britain, the main radio stations are state-run. RTBF1 ("La une," 96.1 FM) and VRT1 (91.7 FM) offer mixed programming. Radio 21 (99.1 FM) is Francophone Belgium's equivalent of the U.K.'s Radio 1, pumping out current chart music, recent releases, dance, and indie music. The Flemish version is StuBru (Studio Brussel) 100.6 FM which offers a trendsetting blend of rock, house, and techno sounds. Bruxelles Capitale radio (99.3 FM) features music that is more mainstream with a fair sprinkling of oldies and French chanson. The Flemish version is Radio Donna (88.3 FM). Nostalgie (100.0 FM) shows you what Francophone Belgians consider "classic hits" while Air Libre (87.7 FM), run by the North African community, plays plenty of rai. Reception of the BBC World Service is reasonably clear on 648kHz MW with programming in both English and German. For classical music, try Musique 3 (91.2 FM).

Alternatives in other regions include VRT Radio 3 (89.5 FM), France Musique (99.4 or 88.7 FM), Holland 4 (98.7 FM) and the German station WDR3 (95.1 FM). Note that frequencies given here are for Brussels but vary considerably in different regions. Details are found in the weekly *Télé Moustique* magazine.

In Belgium, car radios incur an annual license fee of 1092BEF/ year. There is no such fee for a radio kept at home.

LITERATURE

For Belgian writers, the nature of the linguistic divide tends to ensure that their popularity is limited to one or the other language community. Flemish writers might seek fame and fortune in the Netherlands and Francophone Belgians, in France. A notable example is Georges Simenon (1903–1989) whose Maigret is the classic detective character in French literature, though Simenon himself was Belgian. Despite his demure, pipe-in-hand appearance, Simenon is said to have bedded more women than Bill Clinton and David Mellor put together— 10,000, by his own modest estimate. If you're interested in doing a Simenon tour of Liège, start at his birth place, 24 Rue Léopold. Other Francophone literary greats include playwright Michel de Ghelderôde (1898–1962), Antwerp-born poet Emile Verhaeren (1855–1916) and Camille Lemonnier (1844–1913), Zola-influenced founder of the so-called Belgian Literary Renaissance. More recently acclaimed authors include Françoise Mallet-Joris and Jacqueline Harmpan (Prix Medicis for Orlanda in 1996).

Hendrik Conscience (1812–1883) is an interesting Belgian literary figure of the 19th century. A prolific sentimental historical novelist and short story writer, he is credited with the development of the Flemish novel, even though his father was French-speaking and he himself started out writing Francophone poetry. His most famous works are *In't Wonderjaar* (a series of 16th century historical life sketches) and *De Leeuw van Vlaanderen* (*The Lion of Flanders*). The latter tells the story of the Battle of the Golden Spurs in 1302. Its publication in 1838 was an important rallying point for Flemish nationalism, while the much later film version directed by Hugo Claus is hilariously Monty Pythonesque.

At the turn of the century, the Flemish literature movement was an important source of renewed community pride. Leading figures were Guido Gezelle (1830–1899), Herman Teirlinck (1879–1967), and Frank Lateur (1871–1961), who wrote under the appropriately Flemish-sounding pen name Stijn Streuvels and is best known for *De*

Vlaschaard, which was written in 1907. Priest and poet, Gezelle wrote direct simple evocations of religious and rural life and was posthumously adopted as a literary icon by Flemish nationalists. His centenary in 1999 was very widely celebrated in Flanders. Sculptures of Gezelle are considered "accurate" if the skin is suitably lumpy and the head oversized—he was hydrocephalic "with such a surfeit of brains that he had constant headaches".

Twentieth century Flemish writer Hugo Claus was short-listed for the Nobel Literature Prize for *Het Verdriet van België*—which translates as The Sorrow of Belgium. The title refers not to the depressing weather but to a phrase the hero's mother uses to describe her son. The book is a masterpiece exploring the stoical Belgian character through a portrayal of life under Nazi occupation (1939–1945). Its use of archaic, yokel, and French terms (retained when possible in the English translation), is an integral element of the book's satire on Flemish nationalism.

The Flemish equivalent of the Booker Prize is the Libris while Francophone writers aspire to the Prix Rossel, Prix Medicis, or even toward the Grand Prix of France's National Academy. *Stupeur et Tremblements* won the latter in 1999 for Amélie Nothomb, a prolific young Francophone Belgian authoress born in Kobé, Japan to a diplomatic family.

NEWSPAPERS

De Standaard is the most stridently Flemish nationalist newspaper. *La Libre Belgique* (started during World War II as a secret underground newspaper) is a French daily with a perceived upper-class readership and a firmly "keep-Belgium-united" stance.

De Morgen, *La Dernière Heure*, and *Het Laatste Nieuws* are progressive-liberal newspapers, each with a relatively lowbrow populist tone. Curiously, considering the Belgian love of gossip, there are no real muck-raking tabloid newspapers— "we don't have a culture for them," said one Belgian friend without a hint of irony. *Le Soir* is a respected Francophone daily. It contains a useful cultural supplement on Wednesdays and has good on-line news archives at http://www.lesoir.com/. Other regional newspapers include *Le Courrier et l'Escaut* in Tournai, *La Wallonie* in Liège, and *Gazet van Antwerpen* in…guess where. *Vlan*, which appears in various local varieties, is a free advertisement listings newspaper which is useful if you're looking to buy or sell anything.

L'Echo and *De Financieel-Ekonomische Tijd* are the Francophone and Flemish business newspapers. Newspapers in English including *The Financial Times*, *The Times*, *Herald Tribune*, and *The Wall Street Journal* are all reprinted locally. Other British and American newspapers are available as imports.

Metro is a free newspaper given away on the Brussels metro and certain mainline trains. Available in French or Flemish it has events and TV listings and gives website links for readers to follow up the news and sports stories reported. Its inspired "Kiss and Ride" column allows love-struck passengers to admit their burning passions for fellow commuters with whom they may only have made brief wordless eye-contact across a crowded carriage. Some entries are quite poetic.

MAGAZINES

Le Vif L'Express and *Knack* are respectively the main Francophone and Flemish news weeklies. Both are respected for their independent political voices.

Tele Moustique is the Francophone Belgian equivalent of the *Radio Times*, a TV guide that advertises itself as "the magazine that bites" (its name translates as TV Mosquito). It earned national respect for its investigative journalism by nibbling away at a series of pedophile and corruption cases and keeping the public focussed on serious allegations when a bout of finger-pointing in 1997 appeared to taint half of the political elite. *Humo* is the Flemish-language equivalent. Considered a master of irony, its present editor Guy

Mortier is also a TV and radio personality. *Trends* is a Flemish business magazine.

Park Mail, a Francophone magazine is given away at—you guessed it—car parks. It's worth picking up for the amusing and sarcastic snipes at recent news events that you'll find on the first page. English-language news weeklies *Time*, *Newsweek*, and *The Economist* are widely available while *The Bulletin* is the best source of Belgian news in English and has a comprehensive weekly events listing.

SPORTS

A sure way to bluster into conversations is through a shared appreciation of sports. In Pakistan, it's cricket and hockey, in Japan, sumo and volleyball, in Papua New Guinea, mini wars. The events that come closest to pushing football from the Belgian sports headlines are Formula One motor racing and cycling.

Cycling

In the first 60 years of the cycling World Championships, Belgians won a phenomenal 22 times. Recent Belgian stars are Johan Museeuw (champion in 1995 and 1996), Frank Vandenbroucke (1999), and Russian-born Belgian Andreï Tchmil, "the lion of Siberia" who won the 1999 World Cup. Arguably the world's most famous cyclist ever was Belgian Eddy Merckx, five times winner of the Tour de France in 1969, 1970, 1971, 1972, and 1974.

But it's not just great sportsmen who share the passion. On Sunday mornings, most towns have a veterans cycling club that consists mostly of pensioners who cycle a substantial circuit, although not, of course, before tucking into a fortifying beer or three. The following are some of the key cycling events:

Le Tour des Flandres one of the 12 stages in the cycling World Cup, held in early April. Its most gruelling stretch is the infamously steep, cobbled slopes of the Mur de Grammont.

La Flèche Wallonne	Charleroi to Huy, in mid-April
La Flèche Brabançonne	late March
Liège–Bastogne–Liège	mid-April
The Gent "six days"	November
The 24-hour cycling tourney at Ciney	August

Motor Racing

Even though local Formula One heroes Jacky Ickx and Thierry Boutsen are no longer racing, Formula One remains extremely popular amongst ordinary Belgians who stay glued to their TV sets until 3 a.m. to see the latest rally live from one of the world's least convenient time zones.

An original blanket ban on tobacco advertising due to be imposed on Jan 1, 1999 caused a great commotion and threatened to bring an end to the beloved Belgian Grand Prix. However, the decision was overruled by the high court allowing a four-year reprieve. So for now the Grand Prix, held every August since 1979 at Francorchamps near Spa, continues to be a favorite sporting event. The course also hosts a classic 24-hour motor rally: a punishing endurance contest like the better-known equivalent at Le Mans (France), which, incidentally, Jacky Ickx won six times.

Football

It's often said that along with the monarchy, Belgium's national team, the Red Devils are one of the main things that keep the nation together. For expatriates itching for a game, British United FC has several teams playing at different levels. To join the club, visit its website at http://www.come.to/bufc.

The best known Belgian soccer clubs are at Anderlecht (an inner city commune of Brussels otherwise associated with Erasmus and ethnic unrest) and FC Brugge of Bruges. Their fans maintain a traditional enmity which erupted in what was dubbed "British-style hooliganism" when the teams met in January 1999. Some 400 seats were ripped up and thrown onto the pitch and Anderlecht fans were subsequently banned from Bruges. Nonetheless, during Euro 2000, co-hosted by Belgium and the Netherlands, it was still the British fans who were considered the most dangerous. The authorities' fear dates back to the traumatic Juventus versus Liverpool European Cup final in 1985 when 39 supporters died in what is now the rebuilt King Baudouin stadium at Heysel (Brussels).

Curious Alternative Sports in Rural Belgium

Balle Pelotte

With a certain similarity to the jai alai (pelota) of the Basque country, *balle pelotte* is a game in which two teams slapping a bouncy powerball toward each other using bare or gloved hands on an open court. Televised on little-watched Belgian provincial channels, the event of a big match is like a rural fête with impromptu bands of three or four gently inebriated musicians serenading the crowd. The irregularly shaped Ballodrome is a court usually a little more than a village square marked with lines and painted oil cans for distance markers.

Animal and Bird Competitions

Recently, the curious sport of pigeon racing hit the headlines when a Belgian fancier's birds were stolen from their dovecotes. The audacity of the theft was shocking, but so too was the discovery that these birds were valued at some 10,000,000BEF! April 2001 brought the offbeat sports story of the year: some 80 pigeon-fanciers were under investigation for suspected doping of their birds with performance enhancing drugs!

And this is not the only popular bird sport. Some eccentric folks in West Flanders spend their Sunday mornings taking their caged finches to the park. In a bizarre competition, the birds are judged for their ability to sing a very specific song. Birds that get it wrong are corrected, although the most stubborn and slow learners are usually released—eventually. There are more than 40,000 competition finches registered in Belgium. There are similar competitions for singing dogs, although these are less uniquely Belgian.

— *Chapter Thirteen* —

CELEBRATIONS
AND EVENTS

The sheer endless variety of folkloric parades as well as exhibitions, shows, festivals, and events in Belgium means that there need never be a weekend without a dozen choices of something new to see. The biggest problem is sifting through the myriad possibilities.

THE YEAR IN OUTLINE

Winter

During the cold months of January and February, indoor activities predominate: there are plenty of trade fairs (homes, cars, travel, antiques, etc.) plus the Brussels International Film Festival. The Fête

193

des Rois Mages (Feast of the Magi) falls on January 6. All over Belgium, households celebrate the late arrival of Jesus' Biblical birthday presents (of gold, frankincense, and myrrh) by eating a special cake into which is baked a "lucky" coin. Increasingly, other novelties are substituted for the coin. In 2000, popular versions of this cake contained a ceramic Tarzan figure for kids to joyfully break their teeth on.

Lenten Festivals

Mardi Gras (the "fat" Tuesday before Lent) is six weeks before Easter. It's the culmination of many days of preliminary festivities in Binche, Belgium's greatest carnival town. The famous Gilles de Binche briefly don their spooky masks at around 11 a.m., then reassemble at 3:30 p.m. for the orange-throwing procession, wearing their exotically quivering ostrich headgear. Being hit by an Gilles-thrown orange is considered a blessing. Throwing one back would be considered extremely offensive.

The honor of being a Gilles de Binche is usually passed from father to son.

Dozens of other towns have carnivals of their own. Aalst's raucous, onion-throwing bonanza is also held during Mardi Gras together with the Voil Jeanetten (Dirty Prostitute) procession of garishly cross-dressed men in giant bras and old corsets carrying broken umbrellas. Eupen's more picturesque Rosenmontag (Rose Monday) is the day before, and other carnivals occur each weekend between Dimanche Gras (e.g. at Malmédy and at Tongeren) and Palm Sunday (at Genappe, a quaintly banal affair of purely local interest).

Binche may have the finest Gilles, but several other towns have their own versions. Stavelot's carnival (fourth Saturday of Lent) is famous for its Blancs Moussis. These are white-capped figures with long-nosed masks, originally donned to protect the participants from the plague. Or, according to another story, so that monks could join in the fun without being noticed. The next day in Tilff, carnival participants wear extraordinary tall green headgear which turns them into giant pineapples while in Hélécine they're dressed as witches. Somewhat more refined is Ostend's Dead Rat Ball, held on the first Saturday of March at the Kursaal Casino. Celebrated since 1898, it is touted as the biggest fancy dress ball in Europe. Book well ahead.

On Ash Wednesday, traditional Walloon villages spend the afternoon in the ancient ritual of *crossage de rue*, which is a sort of golf where a (traditionally wooden) *chôlette* ball is struck with a *rabot* stick, the target usually being in the form of a beer barrel placed in front of a café or bar. You can join the fun in the Hainaut village of Chièvres. Call 068 657 534 for information.

The first Sunday of Lent goes by several names, including the Sunday of *Brandons*, *Escouvillons*, or *Feûreû*. Its climax is the burning of Mr Winter (*le Bonhomme Hiver*) in one of seven bonfires in Bouge, Namur. The folks in the red robes are the "brotherhood of the great fire." If you see people with big batons, these are not for causing crowd trouble but to beat the trees in local orchards—a practice which traditionally was said to bring a good fruit crop.

The spirit of winter is ceremonially torched many times more throughout March, but mostly in rural villages that are seldom visited, such as Orp-leGrand and Walhain in Walloon Brabant. These events are totally un-commercialized and barely known beyond the village limits—a really great way to delve into rural culture.

Spring

By Easter, things have calmed down a little. Children burrow around the garden looking for Easter eggs which are delivered, so they're told, courtesy of the Bells of Rome. If you're looking for a spectacle there's the curious egg-throwing festival at Kruishoutem and an eerie penitents procession at Lessines. Torch-bearing figures at the latter wear costumes resembling monks' habits. A similar procession in late July at Veurne involves the penitents carrying huge crosses around the old town center.

As is common across all of Europe, April 1 is the day of practical jokes. In Belgium, the classic gag is to stick a paper cutout of the *poisson d'avril* fish on someone's back. May 1 is Labor Day, on which it is an almost expected custom for men to present a small posy of *muguet/meiklokje* (lily of the valley) to female friends, family, and colleagues.

Ascension Day is celebrated with a grand cortège of horsemen, archers, and musicians riding through Bruges escorting a 12th century reliquary which supposedly contains a few drops of Christ's blood. The Sunday before is the similarly dramatic Hanswijk procession in Mechelen in which citizens traditionally thank the Virgin Mary for her supposed role in the town's "miraculous" deliverance from the plague in 1272.

Several towns (e.g. Soignies, Wasmes, Gerpines) have religious festivals on Whit Monday. Then six days later on Trinity Sunday, Mons erupts with the brilliant Ducasse de St Waudru featuring the procession of the Car d'Or: a golden carriage which holds the saint's relics. The day culminates in the Lumeçon battle in which St George defeats a dragon with the unfortunate name of Doudou.

There are many other late spring festivities, notably the blessing of the sea at Knokke, *maitrank* drinking in Arlon, the Ros Beiaardommegang medieval pageant in Dendermonde, and the Brussels Jazz Marathon.

Summer

Summer sees a deluge of music festivals and commercial events at the seaside: in the most impressive, part of the beach at Zeebrugge is turned into a gigantic art gallery of enormous sand sculptures. Meanwhile virtually every commune in Belgium has its own summer *braderie*, fête, or fair, though this might be little more than a big car boot sale, perhaps with a couple of minor roundabouts, beignet fryers, shooting stands, and lucky dip stalls around the village square. The biggest is Brussels' Foire du Midi which commandeers half of the Boulevard de Midi for over a month to host an extensive fairground with a reputation for thrills, candy floss, and pickpockets.

National Day (July 21) passes with a military parade but little fanfare. On August 9, a somewhat chaotic cortège of giants and revellers block Brussels city traffic for the planting of the *Meiboom*, which strangely, considering the date, translates as May Tree. The festival is loosely based on a historic conflict involving a wedding party, a saint, and a gang of disruptive youths. Assumption Day falls on August 15 every year. This is the busiest national holiday of all with something happening in almost every town: fireworks, fairs, bathtub races, etc. Aarschot turns off all its electric lights and illuminates itself with thousands of candles. Malmédy scrambles 10,000 eggs for a giant omelette.

On the fourth week of August with the school holidays petering out, David takes on Goliath in the culmination of the Ducasse giants' parade at Ath, a procession dating back to the 15th century.

The Ommegang

The first Thursday in July is the Ommegang, Brussels most dramatic pageant. Soon after the 1348 construction of a chapel at the Sablon, an impoverished cloth worker, Beatrice Soetkens, saw a vision of the Virgin. The apparition, while grateful for the new chapel in her honor, urged Soetkens to furnish it with a much venerated 13th century Madonna statuette known as O.L.V. op 't Stokske (Our Lady of the Branch). Convinced, she somehow persuaded her pious husband to row her all the way to Antwerp so that she could steal the figure. Her adventure proved remarkably successful and the sheer bizarre audacity of the mission made it seem almost a miracle. God's will, it seemed, had paralysed all those who tried to stop her, and, once when the poor husband collapsed with exhaustion at the oars, the Lord even deigned to blow the couple's boat back to Brussels. Given such obvious divine intervention, even the Antwerp authorities decided to accept the *fait accompli*. In Brussels the mysterious myth became the focus for a great procession in which the statuette was displayed by walking it around the city: hence *Ommegang*, (*omme* = around, *gang* = walk).

Over the years, the Ommegang has evolved beyond recognition. In its 20th century form, the main focus is no longer the Virgin statuette, but an impressive evocation of Charles V and Philip II's Joyeuse Entrée of 1549. In full medieval garb, the pair is flanked by standard-bearers on horseback, heralds, pages, and nobles mixed in with a hotchpotch of Gilles, Giants, and Merchtem waterbirds. Real historical characters from the original Entrée are represented, right down to the royal pets. "Charles" carries the emblem of the Golden Fleece. Some of the characters are played by the direct descendants of Charles' original noble entourage. The day culminates in fireworks and a great costume ball. You need a ticket to attend the finale (book well in advance through the Brussels Tourist Information Bureau at 02 513 8320). The website http://www.ommegang-brussels.be/uk/index.htm has more background on the event plus seat prices, various photos, and press clippings.

Sand sculptures on the beach at Zeebrugge. Impressive...until it rains.

Fall

In autumn, things turn alcoholic. In mid-September the boisterous Fêtes de Wallonie give the French-speaking community the excuse to tuck into the lethal *peket* firewater. In Poperinge, there's a hop parade held every three years (2002, 2005). And in mid-October is Hasselt's *jenever* festival. Perhaps as a counterbalance, the beginning of September also heralds the Heritage Days.

Amongst the odder local festivities are Jodoigne's pig festival (second week in October), the intriguing "Day of the Edible Landscape" at Bokrijk's open-air museum (end of September) and the festival in Mol Ginderbuiten where 100,000 light bulbs illuminate a jolly parade of giants and bands on the evening of the last Saturday of September (but never on the 30th!).

Halloween is a recently imported idea celebrated by trick-or-treating kids but without any real cultural pedigree in Belgium (though the country has plenty of homegrown witch festivals e.g. at Beselare in July). All Saints' Day, on the first of November, is a national holiday which was traditionally the time for visiting family graves. These days most Belgians treat it with their usual irreverence by beetling off somewhere for the long weekend. Only the most pious head for Scherpenheuvel on the first Sunday of November. Armistice Day on the 11th is the time to remember the war dead.

In the week leading up to St Verhaegen's Day (third Friday in November), students in laboratory coats walk the city streets, waving collection buckets at motorists, begging beer money. Actually Verhaegen wasn't a saint at all, but the founder of the Brussels Free University. Avoid central Brussels on St Verhaegen's Day unless you're happy to be plastered with flour and eggs. The first of December is St Eloi's Day, the workers' equivalent of St Verhaegen's Day, where public drunkenness is not only acceptable, it's expected.

Christmas

In some European countries, it's St Nicholas' Day (on December 6)

Even straw gets merry in September!

rather than Christmas on which children receive their presents from a white-bearded old housebreaker who sneaks down the chimney and violates their shoes, stockings, or socks (with presents, that is). Belgian kids are lucky—they receive presents on both days. St Nicholas also donates fancy *speculoos* biscuits. The Santa/ St Nicholas characters sitting in Belgian stores are accompanied by a boot-polished colleague named Pére Fouetard/Zwarte Piet (Black Pete). As in the British tradition Santa asks the child if he/she has been good. And good children get a gift. Bad Belgian children, however, risk not only a reduced cache of presents, but also the wrath of Black Pete, who wields a big club to whack the sinners. Albeit symbolically.

At Christmastime, town centers hold festive markets. A common feature—besides the hot *glühwein* and chocolate truffles—are full-sized Nativity scenes. In some such scenes, the stables are populated with real animals and occasionally there's even a live "Virgin" in attendance with a real baby bawling in the manger. The job can be rather cold, if, like in Anderlecht, it's performed outdoors.

NON-ANNUAL PAGEANTS

Some of the most dramatic pageants do not occur every year, such as Brussels' biannual Tapis Fleuri. The incredibly dramatic Waterloo battle reconstruction is normally held every five years but was cancelled in 2000 to avoid a clash with the Euro 2000 football competition. The following are some other events that do not occur on a yearly basis.

The Golden Tree Pageant	held every five years in Bruges. This is a majestic evocation of the 1468 wedding of Charles the Bold (of Burgundy and Flanders) to the English princess Margaret of York.

Halle's pilgrims' procession	commemorates a legend in which the Virgin Mary appeared in Halle, her face blackened with smoke, when the city was under siege in 1498. Celebrated on Whit Sunday in odd years.
The Kattestoet Festival	since as early as A.D. 932 there's been an odd tradition of hurling live cats off the balcony of the Cloth Hall in Ieper. Some claim that the cats were kept in winter to guard the wool, but

The Tapis Fleuri. Every two years, the Grand Place in Brussels is covered in an incredible patterned carpet of flower petals.

weren't needed in summer so were disposed of. Another explanation links the cat-killing to a symbolic anti-sorcery display. Either way, these days cloth replicas are used instead of live felines and gigantic cats are wheeled around in a procession. Celebrated on the second Sunday in May on odd-numbered years.

St Dympna Ommegang some 2000 players act out a historical pageant related to the 7th century Christian Irish princess Dympna who fled from her incestuous, heathen father, only to end up beheaded in Belgium. Celebrated in Geel in May every five years.

— *Chapter Fourteen* —

WHERE TO GO?

One of the joys of living in Belgium is the sheer ease of going somewhere else. Hop on the Eurostar to London, the Thalys to Amsterdam, or drive to France for a boot-load of cheap wine. But why rush away? There's loads to see in Belgium: medieval town squares, soaring belfries, moated castles, battlegrounds, and the most idiosyncratic collection of museums imaginable. Bruges is arguably the best-preserved medieval city in Europe, and there are plenty of other gems to explore.

HISTORIC TOWN CENTERS
Belgium's towns grew wealthy much earlier than those of many other

European nations. Although the country subsequently suffered considerably from wars, invasions, and town planners, a surprising wealth of medieval architecture has survived and/or has been restored. Even Ieper, almost entirely flattened during World War I, has had its historic center attractively rebuilt. The main cities have beautiful centers, especially Gent, Antwerp, Mons, and Mechelen. Brussels' Grand Place is arguably the most beautiful medieval square in Europe and it's worth seeking out the city's brilliant Art Nouveau treasures—a special pleasure since many of the best host atmospheric café and bars. St Truiden, Tienen, Tournai, Grimbergen, and Enghien are other particular delights but a personal top five would be:

Bruges	brilliantly preserved with a myriad of attractive canal views
Lier	less extensive than Bruges but with less bustle
Zoutleeuw	visit the Charles V town hall and the extraordinary architecture of the St Leonard's Church around the square of a small, formerly walled town
Tongeren	Belgium's oldest town
Leuven	lively student atmosphere and splendid Gothic town hall

BELFRIES AND CURIOUS CLOCKS

In the Middle Ages, the height and grandeur of a town's belfry tower was a symbol of a town's prosperity and independence. Many still stand, especially in Flanders. In 1999, UNESCO recognized Belgium's 30 great belfries as a world heritage collection. Eye-catching examples include those at Aalst, Bruges, Mons, Lier, and St-Truiden.

The latter two towns also display unique timepieces. The extraordinarily intricate Zimmer tower clock in Lier was built in the early 1930s but looks medieval. In the building next to the St-Truiden's *begijnhof*, you can see "performances" of the Festraets Astronomical Clock, complete with a Foucault Pendulum. If you visit Nivelles, Kortrijk, or Virton, keep an eye on the church towers as the hour approaches. Chimes are rung by intriguing mechanical bell-ringer figurines.

FOUNTAINS

The typically understated Belgian sense of humor is evident in the joy the population takes in dressing the Manneken-Pis up. The minuscule statue of a little boy taking a leak actually owns more than 600 fanciful costumes. His wardrobe is kept in the Maison du Roi city museum at the Grand Place. The original 1619 statuette was stolen and destroyed in 1817 but the smashed pieces were eventually recovered and a new cast made. A spare was constructed in case anyone tries to steal the original again! The lesser-known Jeanneke-Pis is a female equivalent who does her thing at the far end of a little alley off the Petit Rue des Bouchers. Other intriguing fountains include the Hasselt gin barrel (See Chapter Ten) and the 1887 Brabo fountain in Antwerp's Grote Markt, Antwerp. The latter is a gory depiction of the first count of Flanders flinging the severed hand of the giant Antigonus into the river Scheldt—a deed which is the apocryphal derivation for the town's name (*werp* = throw, *ant* = mispronunciation of hand).

CASTLES

There are so many fantastic castles in Belgium that tourist offices sell packs of cards, each one featuring a different château. A large number are well-preserved and dramatically set in well-maintained moats, all spiky with towers. A very condensed list is given below, chosen more for overall visual appearance and atmosphere than for historical merit.

The fairy tale castle of Beersel: peace and tranquillity just three minutes off the Brussels Ring.

Antwerp	Antwerp's Sterckshof Provincial Museum is housed in a very dramatic moated castle
Beersel	conveniently near Brussels, dramatic but unfurnished
Gaasbeek	set in splendid grounds and with luxurious interiors
Bouillon	massive ridge-top fortress of Godfrey, the leader and bankroller of the first Crusade
Harvé	partially restored ruin on a big island
Horst	moated beauty near St Peters Rode
Modave	perched on a cliff, although you wouldn't notice this from the palatial main entry
Namur	extensive citadel and fortress that dominates the town

GREAT RELIGIOUS BUILDINGS

The Belgian abbeys took a hammering after the French Revolution and relatively few retain much of their former grandeur. Those that have been rebuilt are generally rather austere and more interesting for their breweries than for their architecture. However, some outstanding religious structures remain.

To get a sense of its grandeur, Tournai's classic five spired 12th century cathedral is best viewed from the terrace of the Au Vieux Tournay café at the west end of the Grand Place. Nivelles' St Gertrude's and Soignies' Collégiale St Vincent are similarly massive, austere Romanesque structures. Villers-la-Ville's once great abbey

Many otherwise unexciting towns, like this one in Aarschot, are graced with imposing and austere Demergothic churches.

was sacked in 1794 but the atmospheric ruins are protected and used occasionally as the venue for musical or theatrical performances.

The St Leonarduskerk in Zoutleeuw is unique in retaining its incredible pre-Reformation interior and artworks, but is only open from Easter till the end of September between 2 and 5 p.m. Closed on Mondays too! Antwerp's Onze Lieve Vrouw cathedral has a splendid Gothic nave with Baroque embellishments and paintings by Rubens. Aarschot and Halle have fine examples of Demergothic churches with bulbous spires, Walcourt has the onion-domed St Materne basilica while Jodoigne's dilapidated Notre Dame du Marché has a curiously twisted steeple.

Brussels has several attractive churches and the splendid Gothic cathedral of Sts Michel & Gudule, reminiscent of Notre Dame in Paris. There's also the simply huge Koekelberg Basilica. It's the world's fifth biggest church and is really rather ugly. Attempts to make it a national monument have less to do with artistic merit than persuading the federal government to pay for its maintenance and diabolical heating bills.

BEGIJNHOFS/BÉGUINAGES

In the 13th and 14th centuries, many women in Flanders were accommodated in protective cloisters. Initially the *begijnhofs* (*beguinages* in French) welcomed women of all classes, and most notably the lonely wives of crusaders who needed protection while their warrior husbands were killing infidels abroad. Unlike nuns, these women didn't have to take permanent chastity or poverty vows, but could retreat from the harsh predatory world to a life of relative contemplative calm. They passed their days developing the art of lace-making. Later the institutions became more like religious poor-houses. Gent still has an active *begijnhof*. Many other Flemish towns—such as Antwerp, Bruges, Diest, Kortrijk, Lier, St Truiden, and Tongeren—have retained at least part of these complexes which make delightful spots for a stroll. The Leuven *begijnhof* is now used as student accommodation.

211

SPA AND FRANCORCHAMPS

Not quite city or countryside, what sleepy Spa lacks in visual appeal it makes up for with curious historical connections and events. Spa is *the* original spa town. It was here that Kaiser Wilhelm signed the armistice ending World War I. And it was in Spa's Hotel du Midi, that King Leopold II's estranged wife Maria-Henrietta took refuge for seven years. Despite its casino, Spa is a fairly sleepy place most of the year, coming alive for the "Francofolies" festival, and for car rallies at nearby Francorchamps including the Belgian Formula One Grand Prix.

BATTLEGROUNDS

Caught between its powerful neighbors, Belgium has long been the unlucky venue for foreigners' wars. Most famously, Napoleon met his Waterloo at, well Waterloo. Neutrality in World War I didn't stop Belgium being pounded into the mud so severely that the fields of Flanders are associated primarily with trench warfare and not feeding milk cows. World War II was every bit as traumatic as the country had to deal with German occupation and aerial bombardment from both sides. Today the sad legacies of these and other battles hold a curious attraction for visitors. But to make a visit to a battlefield interesting, one really needs a good guide to make sense of what are, after all, simply fields.

Waterloo

The battlefield is about five kilometers (three miles) south of Waterloo town by bus W (which starts from Place Roupe in Brussels). The battlefield topography is interesting once one realizes the significance of what at first appears to be a very understated, gentle slope. It was this feature that fooled the advancing French infantry, who hadn't expected to find Wellington's redcoats hiding behind a now disappeared hedgerow on the little ridge. In the lee of a huge artificial memorial hill topped with a bronze lion is a museum whose displays

The Waterloo Battle Memorial. Technically the battlefield now falls just outside the Waterloo commune boundary. But nobody really considers renaming it the Battle of Braine l'Alleud.

glorify Napoleon to the extent that you begin to wonder who actually won! The balance is redressed at the Wellington museum in central Waterloo.

Ramillies

In 1706, the British commander Duke of Marlborough, with the help of Dutch and Danish troops, decimated a French force and prevented its attack on Namur. Howard Green's 1976 book *Cockpit of Europe* helps visitors make sense of the rather widely spread battlefield sights near Taviers, some 25 km (15 miles) north of Namur.

Fontenoy

Three kilometers (1.8 miles) from Ramecroix off the Tournai–Mons Road is the site where a British force impeded a French attack on the Spanish Netherlands (Belgium). French commander Marshal Saxe was hardly helped by the arrival of his King Louis XV who turned up to watch with a vast foppish entourage of wig makers, clock winders, shoe-shiners, and a myriad other useless hangers on. There's a curious monument to Irish soldiers who were, at the time, fighting with the French against the Brits.

Kortrijk/Courtrai

The 1302 Battle of the Golden Spurs (See Chapter Two) was fought less than a kilometer from Kortrijk's Grote Markt. The exact site is now lost within the town sprawl and was around a stream which has since disappeared beneath the Groeningelaan road. Nonetheless, Kortrijk organizes a Golden Spurs festival in early July.

World War I

In a small area of Flanders, many lost their lives with 65,000 missing in action. Their names are recorded on the Menin Gate (Menentoren) and dozens of smaller memorials and graveyards in the region.

Passchendaele (now spelt *Passendale*), one of the most emotive of the battlefields, is marked by the Crest Farm Memorial commemorating Canadians who bloodily regained the ridge in 1917. In Mesen (Messines) ANZAC day is still commemorated, remembering the heavy Kiwi troop casualties here. Overgrown, shell-pocked World War I fortresses remain in Liège Province including Fort le Loncin whose ammo store was exploded on August 15, 1914 taking with it most of the occupants.

World War II

Fought in 1944, the "Battle of the Bulge" was not so named for a fat commander on a mission to slim. With World War II coming to a climax, Hitler had made a last-ditch counter attack and divided the advancing Allied lines with a "bulge" of German forces pushing into the Ardennes. These troops encircled the U.S. 101st Airborne Division at Bastogne. When asked to surrender, commander McAuliffe (now commemorated by a statue and a tank) retorted with the abrupt and much quoted response, "Nuts!". To celebrate this outburst, the Bastogne has adopted a walnut-throwing ceremony in early December. The area where the fighting raged is very extensive, but the Historical Centre in Bastogne can help define the boundaries.

ROYAL EXHIBITS

If you're really interested in the Belgian royal family, there's a dynastic museum in Brussels and visits to the Royal Palace in Brussels are possible in the summer. On Sunday afternoons, All Saints' Day, and special occasions (like the death anniversaries of the kings), the public is allowed to visit the crypt at Laeken Royal Castle, the last resting place of the Belgian monarchs. It's free. Crowds flock to view the botanical collection in the great Art Nouveau royal conservatory which is open briefly to the public in the last week of April or the first week of May. Check at the tourist offices for details.

MUSEUMS: BELGIUM'S WEIRD COLLECTIONS

Belgium is graced with some truly splendid museums. The fine arts collections in each of the main cities are remarkable: Tervuren's African museum offers a fascinating colonial cameo, and the Brussels war museum has an unrivalled collection of military memorabilia if you're into that sort of thing. There are many open-air museums and wildlife parks. Antwerp's zoo is internationally famous. Almost every town down to the smallest commune has a local museum explaining some facet of local culture, demonstrating the art of local crafts, or displaying historical mementoes. Many are endearingly quaint as much for the dedication and love of their curators as for the museums themselves, although come closing time, you're likely to hear a very unambiguous rustling of keys.

Specialist Mini Museums

Belgium's sheer overload of specialist mini museums is quite exceptional. The strangest museum has to be Brussels' Museum of Veteri-

The Schindler elevator museum. Like several of Belgium's more idiosyncratic museums, just managing to get in is a large part of the fun.

216

nary Medicine (45 rue des Vétérinaires) with its stomach-churning collection of skulls and pickled organs, from dogs' prostates to a TB afflicted parrot's head. There is even a horse torso—stuffed with a new born foal—designed for midwifery practice. All this, set in the Neo-renaissance former Cureghem Veterinary School, makes for a very surreal experience.

In a quiet Brussels street, you can visit a Schindler Museum that has nothing to do with lists or the Holocaust. It houses a display of passenger lift apparatuses, and is hidden away in the premises of the eponymous Schindler company which built them. If that's whetted your appetite, here's a further selection from Belgium's encyclopedic catalogue of oddities. Note that some have extremely limited opening times. For example the harness-making museum in Ellezelles only opens 2–6 p.m. on the first Sunday in the months from April to October.

Bakery	Masseik, Aywaille
Barbers	Sint-Niklaas
Bee-keeping	Kalmthout, Tilff
Beer	*See Chapter Ten*
Biscuit boxes	Opheylissem
Blacksmithery	Ittre
Brush	Izegem
Glass	Seraing, Charleroi, Liège
Ham	La Roche-en-Ardenne
Harnesses	Ellezelles
Heraldry	Temse
Hops	Poperinge
Hosiery	Quevaucamps
Iguanodon	Bernissart
Lace	Kortrijk, Brussels
Leather	Peruwelz
Masks	Binche

Nativity cribs	Manderfeld
Playing cards	Turnhout
Processions	Mons
Ribbons	Comines
Roots	Amel
Strawberries	Wépion
Taxidermy	Turnhout
Textiles	Oelegem
Tobacco	Wervik , Harelbeke, Vressesur-Semois
Traditional Flemish buildings	Bokrijk
Weapons	Liège, Brussels

THEME PARKS

Belgium boasts several theme and adventure parks of which the best known was probably Walibi (near Wavre), now renamed 6 Flags. In 1997, a car running along Walibi's 360° loop-the-loop ride suffered a mechanical failure and left its passengers dangling upside down for over half an hour. Fortunately, everyone was strapped in securely. But it was a major blow to its public relations: the park's advertising jingle was rapidly reworded as the popular joke version: "Walibi-bi-bi, *tête en bas bas bas*" ("Walibi-bi-bi, head hangs down-down-down").

PORTS AND WATERWAYS

The port of Antwerp is Europe's second largest port (after Rotterdam). One certainly couldn't call it beautiful, but the sheer scale of it is impressive.

The amazing lock gate systems serving the waterways of Belgium would be of interest to the engineer-tourist. The four hydraulic boat-lifts on the Canal du Centre between Houdeng and Bracquegnies are considered by some industrial architects to be the horizontal water-way equivalent of the Eiffel Tower. More modern, but as remarkable, is the 1967 *plan incliné* at Ronquières (tours are conducted from May to August only). Here, barges get into a huge, moveable bathtub in which they're wheeled up or down a long 5° slope, achieving a height difference of 67 m (220 feet) and saving dozens of lock gates. The Strépy Thieu boat-elevator achieves an essentially similar aim using a 110 m (361 foot) high rotating carrousel, capable of transporting four ships at a time (two up, two down) through a vertical height of 73 m (240 feet).

BEAUTY SPOTS

It's intriguing to see what Belgians place in this category: a typical selection might include the Zwin's extensive sand-dune nature reserve east of Knokke-Heist, the Signal de Botrange, which is Belgium's highest point, or the Tombeau du Géant, a curl of forested valley in the Ardennes.

None of these do much for me. The popular areas of the Ardennes are either thickly forested with coniferous monoculture, or littered with unexciting holiday homes and caravan parks full of curiously satisfied Dutch tourists. And while the Zwin is a refreshing break from the otherwise concrete blighted strip of coastal towns, it hardly warrants a special journey unless you're a birdwatcher. Personally I prefer the vistas along tree-lined canals (e.g. north of Damme), the majestic beech forest of the Forêt de Soignes/Zoniënwoud (southeast of Brussels) and the rolling hillside patchworks of woods and farmland that you find in small enclaves throughout the central areas of Wallonia (e.g. near Spontin).

Caves

In the Ardennes region there are some curious geological features and several cave systems you can explore. Look for the French term *grottes*, (which can also apply to religious grottoes when graced with a Virgin Mary statue à la Lourdes). You can visit those at Sougné-Remouchamps and at Rochefort. But the Grottes de Han at Han-sur-

The deathbed statue of Everard 't Sercleas needs periodic repairs as superstitious Brussels citizens rub holes into the brass of his right arm.

Lesse, between Namur and Luxembourg, are probably the most impressive caves for a casual visit. Enter by tram.

SUPERSTITIOUS SPOTS

Although Belgians are a generally levelheaded people, they have numerous pilgrimage spots (Banneux, Scherpenheuvel, St Hubert, etc.) and a couple of very celebrated ways to score a free wish. One is to rub the head of the Grand Garde monkey on the wall of Mons town hall. Another is to touch the brass arm of Everard 't Serclaes just across the arched passage from the city hall on Brussels' Grand Place. 'T Serclaes was the celebrated deputy mayor of Brussels who had fought as a military leader against the count of Flanders. Whether or not his 1388 murder was really the work of the lord of Gaasbeek, the people of Brussels burnt down the Gaasbeek castle in revenge.

COUNTRY VILLAGES AND SMALL TOWNS

Belgium is much less noted for its quaint villages than for its historic towns. All too often the soaring church spire and graciously walled, fortified farms are overwhelmed by a preponderance of sturdy, practical but characterless modern brick homes as one village sprawls formlessly into the next. Nonetheless, some of the country villages and small towns are cozy and attractive.. The following are also relatively appealing.

Bouillon	castle town that was sold by Duke Godfrey to pay for the first crusade
Chimay	beer and castle town
Crupet	village that overlooks a picturesque moated manorhouse. Great trout.
Damme	historic and quaint canal-side village popularly visited on a boat trip from nearby Bruges
Dinant	squeezed between cliffs and the river Meuse and overlooked by an extensive fortress. Traffic jams can be off-putting on summer weekends.
Durbuy	based on arguable Francophone definitions, Durbuy is touted as the "world's smallest town," and is still not much bigger than it was in 1331. Only in 2000 did the population reach 10,000. This merited a TV report.
La Roche en Ardennes	castle ruins above a small town on a hilly bend on the river Ourthe

Melin	two examples of unremarkable if pretty villages
and Lô	with fortified farms

OVERNIGHT ACCOMMODATION

As well as hotels, most towns have campsites, B&Bs (known as *chambres d'hôtes/gastenkamers*) and *gîtes/langdelijke verblijven* (self-catering rural accommodation typically rented by the week). There are around 30 youth hostels, costing 400–500BEF for a dorm bed, although several of these operate in summer only.

Especially with *chambres d'hôtes* and *gîtes*, there is a common tendency to quote room prices for one person, assuming a twin-sharing arrangement. Also, you should look very carefully at the supplements list before deciding that the place is a good deal: it is not an uncommon practice to add a considerable fee for stays of only one or two nights.

Hikers' cabins are sometimes available especially in Flanders. They hold up to five people in each cabin and you'll need your own sleeping bag. Get a copy of the useful pamphlet *Trekkershutten in Zuid Nederland en Vlaanderen* from tourist offices.

Brochures given out at tourist offices are not always in English. There are dozens of abbreviations and terms to look out for, but the following are some of the most useful:

French

à partir de	from
avec	with
BS	low season
demi pension	half board (i.e. the additional charge added to the room cost for breakfast and dinner)

HS	high season
pppn/par personne par nuit	per person per night

Flemish

HP	half board
HS	high season
korting	discount (e.g. 10% *kamerkorting vanaf 3e nacht* translates as 10% off from the third night on)
kinderen tot... jaar gratis	free for children under...years old
K/O...	from…
LS	low season
prijzen exclusief waarborgsom	price does not include deposit
toeslag single	supplement for single occupancy
toeslag 1 nacht	supplement for single night occupancy
VP	full board

CULTURAL QUIZ

1000 BEERS ARE BREWED IN BELGIUM, NAME THEM...

TRIGG.

Time for a little fun. Below I describe eight possible situations in which you could conceivably find yourself. Choose the best available response or responses from the choices given. There are no prizes.

SITUATION ONE
You're invited to the home of a married business Belgian colleague for a dinner party. Should you bring:

- **A** Chocolates
- **B** Wine
- **C** Flowers
- **D** Nothing at all

COMMENTS

Any except D—a gift is almost always appropriate. Flowers are specially good for female colleagues or male colleagues' wives.

SITUATION TWO

Late one evening, you're with some friends in a Belgian café and you've just ordered yourself a coffee. One of the half drunken regulars sidles up and asks you if you are Bob. Should you:

- **A** Exclaim, "How did you know?!"
- **B** Edge away, he's attempting a homosexual chat up line
- **C** Agree and point out that you've got a long way to drive home
- **D** Reply, "Robert to you, sir!"

COMMENTS

While none of these may apply, the most appropriate answer is likely to be C as *Bob* refers to the person in a group of drinkers who chooses not to drink alcohol in order to drive home safely. In reality, Bobs and Bobettes are rarer than they should be given the devil-may-care attitudes to drink-driving.

SITUATION THREE

Around Christmastime there's a knock at the door and there's a man claiming to be from the Post Office or Fire Brigade apparently selling a calendar. Do you:

- **A** Buy one
- **B** Call the police
- **C** Check his identification card and offer a small donation
- **D** Complain that you're fed up with salesmen and tell him not to come round again

COMMENTS

Several of the services do send bona fide representatives to collect money for their employees' social clubs. While you're under no obligation to buy a calendar, a donation (i.e. C) shows goodwill and just might be a good investment to stop letters going astray. However, do check the representative's identification documents as there are frequent cases of fakes.

SITUATION FOUR

You're visiting Leuven. You fancy a *pain au chocolat* for breakfast and have located a bakery that sells them. What is the most appropriate thing to say when the attendant comes to serve you?

    A *"Un pain au chocolat s'il vous plaît"*

    B *"Een chokolate broodje alstublieft"*

    C "A *pain au chocolat*, please"

    D *"Goede dag"*

COMMENTS

The most inappropriate choice in a stridently Flemish town like Leuven would be A since French is not at all appreciated there. Many people speak English, so C would probably work. Option B is technically fine, but it's always best to kick off with a little greeting— i.e. D.

SITUATION FIVE

You're driving along the main road when a car squeals out of a side road to your right, turns left straight across your path, narrowly avoiding a crash. Do you:

    A Make chase while shouting obscenities at the idiot

    B Write down the number plate of the offending car and try to find a witness

    C Grumble under your breath about Belgian road sense

    D Slow down and watch more carefully at subsequent junctions

COMMENTS

While C is a probable reaction, D is the only practical course of action as the *priorité à droite* rule means that legally it is *you*, not the driver of the other car, who was being reckless.

SITUATION SIX

You've found a great vantage point where you can sit on a wall to watch a carnival procession. Suddenly you're hit on the side of the head by an orange. You look around in time to see a man in a Tweedledum costume flinging another orange at your face. Do you:

    A Raise your middle finger in a clenched gesticulation meaning "one more"

    B Scream abuse to prevent him throwing another one

    C Wave your arms to make yourself a more obvious target

    D Catch the next orange and playfully lob it back at the thrower

COMMENTS

The only appropriate answer is C. The throwing of oranges during carnivals, while occasionally a little over forceful, represents a gift of semi-religious significance. To throw it back (D) is particularly bad manners. The one finger salute (A) certainly doesn't mean "one more" and is gratuitously offensive. However, raising the first finger is indeed a way that many people in the crowd appeal for more oranges to be thrown at them.

SITUATION SEVEN

A Belgian acquaintance sums up typical Belgian food in a single word: *ballekes*. What does she mean?

A She's describing a typical meatball dish

B She's using a Bruxellois term meaning "rich (i.e. referring to a dish traditionally only served at feasts and formal balls)

C She means that it has a remarkable similarity to the cuisine of the Balkans

D She's adopting a mildly rude expletive. Such slightly coarse language, along with its implied modesty about the country's food, is typically Belgian.

COMMENTS

The meaning of *ballekes* is indeed meatballs and they are typically Belgian. Answer A is thus the nearest possibiliy.

SITUATION EIGHT

Which of the following beers (Leffe, *framboise*, Jupiler, Kwak, Gordon's Highland Scotch) goes with which of the following glasses?

A Round-bottomed glass held upright in a wooden stand

B A glass that tapers slightly from a wider top to a narrower base

C A glass that resembles a thistle

D An oversized wine glass with a heavy bowl and stem

COMMENTS

A with Kwak; B with Jupiler; C with Gordon's Highland Scotch; and D with Leffe. *Framboise* (raspberry beer) would usually be served in a champagne-style flute, i.e. none of the above.

DO'S AND DON'TS
APPENDIX

DO

Do ask questions that show Belgians that you're interested in their country. But watch out for joke answers. Belgian humor, like dry British sarcasm, is not necessarily signalled.

Do restrain yourself if you have strong views on animal rights or the fur trade. Constant criticism of *foie gras* or hunting won't often win you friends.

Do remember that the suicidal *priorité à droite* rule applies to foreigners too!

Do telephone before making an impromptu visit to a Belgian home.

Do be patient (but not to the extent that you get pushed out of queues)

Do support the Red Devils, but don't expect them to win too often.

Do stay calm if someone makes what appears to be a politically incorrect statement.

Do your shopping by Saturday—most shops are closed on Sundays.

Do try ordering tap water in a restaurant: but only if you want to embarrass all your local friends!

DON'T

Don't call French speaking Belgians "French." They will not be flattered!

Don't practise your French in Flanders! It would be much more tactful to speak English.

Don't assume people speak Walloon because they live in Wallonia.

Don't joke about apparently petty or comic displays of linguistic solidarity like De Gordel. They are serious.

Don't imagine that even the most avowed nationalist would really prefer to join France or Holland.

Don't trust pedestrian crossings without very good medical insurance.

Don't assume drivers are sober. As one Belgian motorist put it "If we weren't drunk, we'd be too scared to drive!"

Don't miss the crazy carnivals, the bizarre pageants, and the touchingly banal *braderies*.

Don't admit to Belgian friends that you file your taxes properly. You'll be taken for a liar or a fool.

GLOSSARY

AOC

Appellation d'Origine Controlée: mark awarded to a French wine from a small, carefully defined group of villages if it conforms to that area's specific stylistic and quality guide lines. These are stricter than for a *vin de pays*, which could come from anywhere within a much larger region.

Artois

ancient county of northwestern France, centred on Arras. Artois was passed to Burgundy in 1384 and thence, with Belgium to Spain/Austria in 1493. It has been French again since occupation in 1640, but Stella Artois remains a Belgian beer.

a.u.b

common abbreviation for *please* in Flemish

BEF

commonly adopted abbreviation for Belgian francs. Francs will be replaced by Euro in 2002.

Begijnhof

poorhouse cloister originally built as a retreat for religious women who didn't wish to go the full distance and become nuns. Usually attractive.

Belgae

pre-Roman inhabitants of what is now Belgium

Benelux

Belgium Netherlands Luxemburg. Customs union since 1948, and an economic union from 1960.

Brabançonne	the national anthem, named for the Brabançonne revolt of 1830. The final Flemish version of the words wasn't settled for over a century. Try asking a Belgian to sing it.
Bruxellois	the curious mixed French–Flemish language spoken by certain long-term residents of the capital
BSE	*bovine spongiform encephalopathy* (mad cow disease). Although most publicised cases were in Britain, some sporadic infections were reported in Belgium.
Collégiale	a collegiate church with its own chapter of canons but holding a religious status less than that of a cathedral
Demergothic	architectural style typical of the soaring, bulb spired churches of the Demer river towns
EU	European Union. Brussels is its major bureaucratic hub.
Foreigners	as used by Belgians, this is a generally pejorative term implying non-Europeans. Ironically it might thus include Belgian citizens of Turkish or North African descent, yet exclude Americans, other Western Europeans, and even Japanese.
Honesty	are Belgians honest? In their minds, scrupulously so. There's a great sense of honour and

relatively few would commit what they consider "stealing." Nonetheless, if oversight, technical loopholes, or error fall to one's advantage, a Belgian is most likely to accept that as good luck—don't expect them to return goods delivered by error (they'd have sold them off quickly), and don't suppose that fiddling with taxes count as theft. That's a sport that all are assumed to play.

Huguenots	French Calvinists. Their support for the 16th century Dutch revolts proved insufficient to help deter Spanish interference. The term *Huguenots* may have been derived from the surname of Besançon Hugues, the Calvinist 16th century mayor of Geneva who led the opposition to French annexation of Savoy.
Luncheon Vouchers	a common, legal tax fiddle to disguise part of an employee's salary. Although these vouchers can be used like cash in supermarkets (for food items) or restaurants they don't count fiscally as "pay" because they are officially "purchased" by employees. Yet a 225BEF voucher might only cost 45BEF! So by "selling" them to staff, the company is actually paying 180BEF/day of extra salary tax free!
N. D. de	*Notre Dame de...* = Our Lady of ... Churches are commonly thus prefixed. Flemish equivalent of this would be "O.L.V."
O.L.V op't	*Onze Lieve Vrouw* see *N.D. de* above

OTSI

Office de Tourisme, Syndicat d'Initiative: Francophone citizens advice bureau and tourist office

Pintje

Flemish term for a standard 33 cl glass of draft beer

Police

recently combined into a unified force, the police were formerly divided into commune level police/*politie* and the national gendarmerie/*rijkswacht*. The lack of communication between the two was legendary.

Queuing

despite some claims to the contrary, Belgians are not great queuers. If there's a clear queuing system, they'll stick fairly faithfully to it, and woe betide anyone who tries to push ahead of his/her turn in a shop. But where there can be any sense of ambiguity, the Belgian will be quick to use the excuse to get ahead, i.e. step aside for a moment and you'll lose your place.

Rode

from *rooien*, i.e. to clear forest. For some reason, this deforestation was often carried out in the name of a saint, hence the names of various towns, including St-Pieters Rode and St-Genesius-Rode.

RTBF

Radio Television Belge de la Communaute Francaise—the Francophone Belgian state TV and radio company

RTL   Radio TV Luxembourg

Sabena   Belgian national airline, founded in 1923 as Societé Anonyme Belge d'Exploitation de la Navigation Aérienne

s.v.p   common abbreviation for *please* in French

Time   Belgium runs on Central European time along with most of the EU, an hour ahead of the U.K.

Tipping   in restaurants, bars, and taxis, service charges are always included so tipping is not expected (although taxi drivers try to claim otherwise). In a hairdresser's shop one should tip everyone involved (separate people may cut, wash, perm, etc.) except when the person serving you is the owner. In most theaters and cinemas you're expected to tip the usherette 20BEF. The terms *pourboire inclus/fooi inbegrepen* translate as tip included.

Toilets   Men (*hommes/heren*), Women (*dames/damen*). While most cafés and hotels have toilets, department stores, exhibitions, and many other places with public conveniences often have an old woman lurking at the entrance expecting 10BEF to use the facilities.

White marches   a phenomenon of the late 1990s when whole communities marched in the streets to protest against the lack of action in the aftermath of a string of paedophile murder cases

Witches	although Halloween is not a popular festival, there are witch marches in Nieuwpoort and Beselare
Vin de table	generic, cheap wine that doesn't qualify for AOC or even *vin de pays* status, and may be a blend of wines from unspecified vineyards
Vlaams/ Vlaanderen	Flemish (language)/Flanders in Flemish
VRT	Vlaams Radio-en Televisieomroep: the Flemish state TV and radio company
VTM	Vlaamse Televisie Maatschappij: Flemish private TV and radio company
VVV	Flemish citizens advice and tourist info office

USEFUL WORDS AND PHRASES

English	French	Flemish
Hello	*Bonjour*	*Hallo*
Hi	*Salut*	*Dag*
How do you do	*Comment allez-vous*	*Hoe gaat het met U*
Very good thanks OR	*Très bien merci*	*Zeer goed, dank U*
How are you	*Comment ça va?*	*Hoe gaat het?*
Fine thanks	*Ça va bien, merci*	*Goed, dank U*
How's it going?	*Ça va?*	*Hoe gaat het?*
OK	*Ça va*	*Alles goed*
Good day	*Bonjour*	*Goed dag*

	Bonne journée (said as a farewell)	
Good morning		*Goedemorgen*
Good afternoon		*Goede-namiddag*
Good evening	*Bonsoir*	*Goede avond*
	Bonne soirée (said as a farewell)	
Good night	*Bonne nuit*	*Goede nacht*
Good bye	*Au revoir*	*Tot ziens*
Come back soon	*Reviens vite*	*Kom snel terug*
See you later	*A bientôt*	*Tot later*
Take care	*Fait gaffe* (very colloquial)	*Houd U goed*
Yes	*Oui*	*Ja*
No	*Non*	*Nee*
Maybe	*Peut-être*	*Misschien*
Please	*S'il vous plaît*	*Alstublieft*
Thank you very much	*Merci beaucoup*	*Dank u wel*
Thanks	*Merci*	*Bedankt*
Excuse me	*Excusez-moi*	*Excuseer mij*
I'm sorry	*Je suis désolé(e)*	*Het spijt mij*
How much is that?	*Ça fait combien?*	*Hoeveel maakt dit?*
I	*Je/j'*	*Ik*
Me	*Moi*	*Mij*
My	*Mon/Ma*	*Mijn*
You (informal)	*Tu/Te*	*Jij*
You (formal)	*Vous*	*U*
Your (informal)	*Ton/Ta*	*Jouw*
Your (formal)	*Votre*	*Uw*
He	*Il*	*Hij*
Him	*Lui*	*Zijn*
His/hers	*Son/Sa*	*Haar*

She/her	*Elle*	*Zij*
It	*Il/Elle*	*Het*
Us	*Nous*	*Wij*
Our	*Notre*	*Ons/onze*
They	*Ils/Elles*	*Zij*
It's…	*C'est…*	*Dat is …*
Is it … ?	*Est-ce que c'est…?*	*Is dat…?*
It isn't…	*Ce n'est pas ….*	*Dat is niet …*
Delicious	*Delicieux*	*Lekker*
Good (food)	*Bon*	*Goed*
Good (other)	*Bien*	*Goed*
Beautiful	*Beau/Belle*	*Mooi*
Interesting	*Interesant(te)*	*Interessant (e)*
Strange	*Étrange*	*Vreemd(e)*
Too big	*Trop grand(e)*	*Te groot*
Too small	*Trop petit(e)*	*Te klein*
Too expensive	*Trop cher(e)*	*Te duur*
Early	*Tôt*	*Vroeg(e)*
Late	*Tard*	*Laat(e)*
Fast	*Vite*	*Snel(le)*
Slow	*Lent*	*Traag (trage)*
Very	*Très*	*Erg*
Where is…?	*Où est…?*	*Waar is…?*
Which direction?	*Quelle direction?*	*Welke richting?*
Straight on	*Tout droit*	*Rechtdoor*
Left	*À gauche*	*Links*
Right	*À droite*	*Rechts*
(Not) far from here	*(Pas) loin d'ici*	*(Niet) ver van*
The post office	*La poste*	*Het postkantoor*
The town hall	*La maison communale*	*Het stadhuis*

The tourist office	*L'office de tourisme*	*Het toerismebureau*
The main square	*La grand place*	*De grote markt*
The station	*La gare*	*Het station*
The bus stop for …	*L'arrêt d'autobus vers…*	*…De bushalte*

Shops	*Magasins*	*Winkels*
Bakery	*Boulangerie*	*Bakkerij*
Cake shop	*Pâtisserie*	*Patisserie*
Butcher	*Boucherie*	*Slagerij*
Market	*Marché*	*Markt*
Bookshop	*Librairie*	*Boekenwinkel*
Library	*Bibliothèque*	*Bibliotheek*
Bank	*Banque*	*Bank*
Supermarket	*Supermarché*	*Grootwarenhuis*
Pharmacy	*Pharmacie*	*Apotheek*
Toilet	*Toilette*	*Toilet*

NUMBERS

Numeral	French	Flemish
1	*Un/une*	*Een*
2	*Deux*	*Twee*
3	*Trois*	*Drie*
4	*Quatre*	*Vier*
5	*Cinq*	*Vijf*
6	*Six*	*Zes*
7	*Sept*	*Zeven*
8	*Huit*	*Acht*
9	*Neuf*	*Negen*
10	*Dix*	*Tien*
11	*Onze*	*Elf*

12	*Douze*	*Twaalf*
13	*Treize*	*Dertien*
14	*Quatorze*	*Veertien*
15	*Quinze*	*Vijftien*
16	*Seize*	*Zestien*
17	*Dix-sept*	*Zeventien*
18	*Dix-huit*	*Achttien*
19	*Dix-neuf*	*Negentien*
20	*Vingt*	*Twintig*
21	*Vingt-et-un*	*Eenentwintig*
22	*Vingt-deux*	*Tweeëntwintig*
23	*Vingt-trois*	*Drieëntwintig*
30	*Trente*	*Dertig*
40	*quarante*	*Veertig*
50	*cinquante*	*Vijftig*
60	*Soixante*	*Zestig*
70	*Septante*	*Zeventig*
80	*Quatre-vingt*	*Tachtig*
90	*Nonante*	*Negentig*
100	*Cent*	*Honderd*
101	*Cent-et-un/*	*Honderd en één*
	Cent-et-une	
102	*Cent-deux*	*Honderd en twee*
200	*Deux cents*	*Twee honderd*
300	*Trois cents*	*Drie honderd*
1000	*Mille*	*Duizend*
10,000	*Dix-mille*	*Tien duizend*
100,000	*Cent-mille*	*Honderd duizend*
1,000,000	*Un million*	*Een miljoen*

What's the time?	*Quelle heure est-il?*	*Hoe laat is het?*
One o'clock	*Une heure*	*Eén uur*
Half past two	*Deux heures et demi*	*Half drie*

Quarter past four	*Quatre heures et quart*	*Kwart over vier*
7:20 a.m.	*Sept heures vingt*	*Zeven uur twintig*
7:20 p.m. (19:20)	*Dix-neuf heures vingt*	*Negentien uur*
Twenty to seven	*Sept heures moins vingt*	*Twintig voor zeven*

DAYS OF THE WEEK

English	French	Flemish
Monday	*Lundi*	*Maandag*
Tuesday	*Mardi*	*Dinsdag*
Wednesday	*Mecredi*	*Woensdag*
Thursday	*Jeudi*	*Donderdag*
Friday	*Vendredi*	*Vrijdag*
Saturday	*Samedi*	*Zaterdag*
Sunday	*Dimanche*	*Zondag*

MONTHS OF THE YEAR

English	French	Flemish
January	*Janvier*	*Januari*
February	*Février*	*Februari*
March	*Mars*	*Maart*
April	*Avril*	*April*
May	*Mai*	*Mei*
June	*Juin*	*Juni*
July	*Juillet*	*Juli*
August	*Août*	*Augustus*
September	*Septembre*	*September*
October	*Octobre*	*October*
November	*Novembre*	*November*
December	*Décembre*	*December*

SOME BRUXELLOIS WORDS AND PHRASES

Brol	stuff, things
Chârel	a genius
Chouke/Chikske	darling
Dikke Papzak	fatso
Echte Brusseleirs	real Bruxellois
Façade klasher	a classic insult, now used with humour. The term literally means bad painter referring to Hitler and his lack of talent as an artist.
Fieu	mate, old chap (from *mon vieux*)
Fieutje	my friend/mate
Godverdoem	bloody hell
Jeannette	gay/homosexual
	Note that *voeile jeannette* by contrast means slag/whore (female)
Schuun	attractive
Schuunmeike	cute babe (nice looking young woman)
Schuune brol	cool stuff
Skhieve lavbo	literally twisted toilet. A classic if archaic term of abuse.
Spinnekop	spider
Tich (tish)	penis
Tishke	literally little penis, meaning young lad
Tof	good, cool
Tout près	literally very near in the French language. When appended to a Bruxellois phrase it's effectively meaningless. A bit like *you know* or ...*like*, often added to willy-nilly sentences in English.
Zoug	someone who goes on and on at needless length
Zwanze	joke
Zwanzeur	joker
Zot	twit

For more Bruxellois gems read Roger Kervin de Marke ten Driessche's classic Marollian fables: *Les Fables de Pitje Schramouille* which has recently been republished by Editions Labor.

VARIANT NAMES OF REGIONS

English	French	Flemish
Antwerp	Anvers	Antwerpen
Flemish Brabant	Brabant Flamand	Vlaamse Brabant
Walloon Brabant	Brabant Wallon	Waals Brabant
East Flanders	Flandre Orientale	Oost Vlaanderen
West Flanders	Flandre Occidentale	West Vlaanderen
Hainaut	Hainaut	Hainaut
Limburg	Limbourg	Limburg
Liège	Liège	Luik
Luxembourg	Luxembourg	Luxemburg
Namur	Namur	Namen

VARIANT NAMES OF TOWNS

Flemish Towns

Town	French equivalent
Aalst	Alost
Antwerpen	Anvers
Borgloon	Looz
Brugge	Bruges
De Haan	Le Coq
De Panne	La Panne
Dendermonde	Termonde
Diksmuide	Dixmude
Gent	Gand (Ghent in English)
Halle	Hal
Ieper	Ypres

Mechelen	Malines
Jezus-Eik	Notre-Dame-au-Bois
Kortrijk	Courtrai
Leuven	Louvain
Lier	Lierre
Mesen	Messines
Oudenaarde	Audenarde
Roeselare	Roulers
Ronse	Renaix
Sint-Truiden	St-Trond
Veurne	Furnes
Tienen	Tirlemont
Tongeren	Tongres
Zoutleeuw	Léau

Francophone Towns

Town	**Flemish equivalent**
Ath	Aat
Braine l'Alleud	Eigenbrakel

      (amusingly mispronounced as
        Eigen braaksel = "your own vomit")

Braine le Château	Kasteelbrakel
Braine-le-Comte	's Gravenbrakel
Enghien	Edingen
Huy	Hoeï
Mons	Bergen
Jodoigne	Geldenaken
La Hulpe	Terhulpen
Liège	Luik (Lüttich in German)
Namur	Namen
Nivelles	Nijvel
Saintes	Sint Renelde

Soignies	Zinnik
Tournai	Doornik
Tubize	Tubeke
Waremme	Borgworm
Wavre	Waver

Many more villages have alternative names which have now been largely forgotten but appear on maps from the 1920s and earlier.

RIVERS

Flemish	French
Ijzer	Yser
Leie	Lys
Maas	Meuse
Schelde	Escaut

BEYOND BELGIUM

English	Flemish	French
Aachen	Aken	Aix-la-Chapelle
The Hague	Den Haag	La Haye
Lille	Rijsel	Lille
Lorraine	Lotharingen	Lorraine
Paris	Parijs	Paris
Gravelines	Grevelingen	Gravelines
Dunkirk	Duinkerke	Dunkerque

GEOGRAPHICAL AREAS

Ardennes	southeasterly hill country
Borinage	mining zone of southern Wallonia
Fagnes	hill country stretching from Couvin to the Hautes Fagnes in eastern Wallonia
Famenne	central Wallonia
Gaume	area around Virton

Houtland	"the wooded land" around Tienen even though it's now almost completely deforested
Kempen	flat heathlands of eastern Flanders. Campine in French
Maasland	far eastern Flanders on the Dutch border
Meetjesland	meaning land of the little meadows, or the area around Eeklo
Pays de Herve	cheese country east of Liège
Pajottenland	southwest of Brussels
Waasland	area around Sint Niklaas
Westhoek	far western Belgian Flanders around Ieper

CHRISTIAN NAMES

Though the newer "soap opera" names are not language specific, traditionally many Christian names have different forms in French, Flemish and English. With people you meet, there's no need to attempt a translation. But with monarchs, historical figures, and especially saints (and thus church names) it can be useful to know each form. While some are very similar (Nicholas and Niklaas, Marie and Maria) some are much more divergent, e.g.:

French	Flemish	English
Arnaud	Arend	Arnold
Baudouin	Boudewijn	Baldwin
Catherine	Katelijn	Catherine
Charles	Karel	Charles
Étienne	Steven	Steven
François	Frans	Francis
also as Tchantchès in Liège Walloon, and Susse/Sus/Suske in Bruxellois		
Gaspard	Kasper	Casper
Géoffroi	Godfried	Godfrey
Georges	Joris, George	George

Géry	Gorik	
Gudule	Goedele	
Guillaume	Willem	William
Jacques	Jacob	James
Jean	Jan, Johannes, Hans	John
Jeanne	Johanna, Hanna	Jane/Joanna/Hanna
Laurent	Laurens	Lawrence
Louis	Lodewijk	Louis/Ludwig
Philippe	Filip	Philip
also Flupke in Bruxellois		
Pierre	Pieter, Petrus	Peter
Yves	Ivo	

CALENDAR OF FESTIVALS AND HOLIDAYS

FIXED PUBLIC HOLIDAYS

New Year	January 1
Labor Day	May 1
Flemish Community Day	July 11 (not in Wallonia)
National Day	July 21
Assumption	August 15
Walloon Community Day	September 27 (not in Flanders)
All Saints' Day	November 1
Armistice Day	November 11
Christmas Day	December 25

MOVEABLE FEASTS

	In 2002	**In 2003**
Carnival Sunday/Dimanche Gras	February 10	March 2
Rosenmontag/ Lundi Gras	February 11	March 3
Mardi Gras/Shrove Tuesday	February 12	March 4
Ash Wednesday	February 13	March 5
Quadragésime/1st Sunday of Lent	February 17	March 9
Laetare/Fourth Sunday of Lent	March 10	March 30
Palm Sunday	March 24	April 13
Good Friday	March 29	April 18
Easter Sunday	March 31	April 20
Easter Monday	April 1	April 21
Ascension	May 9	May 29
(*always a Thursday*)		
Whit Sunday (Pentecost)	May 19	June 8
Whit Monday	May 20	June 9
Trinity Sunday	May 26	June 15

RESOURCE GUIDE

EMERGENCY NUMBERS

100	Medical emergency
101	Police
105	Red cross/24-hour ambulance
112	Fire brigade
110	Child Focus (European centre for missing children)
02 648 4014	Community Help Line: offering 24-hour help in English for problems of any kind.
02 512 0505	AIDS Helpline in English, 7–9 p.m. only.

Directory Assistance

Dial 1405 for assistance in English, but beware that the charge is 30/48BEF per min for national/international queries. Ouch. **SCOOT** is a toll free commercial service finder. The website http://www.infobel.com conducts White and Yellow Pages directory searches.

USEFUL WEBSITES

Government website	http://www.belgium.fgov.be
Belgian politics	http://www.political.resources.net/belgium.htm
Belgian search	http://www.advalvas.be/search&find/
Francophone community	http://www.cfwb.be
Flemish community	http://www.flanders.be
Germanophone community	http://www.euregio.nrt/rdg
Brussels Capital region	http://www.bruxelles.irisnet.be

Le Soir (Francophone news)   http://www.lesoir.be
Expatriate information   http://www.xpats.com
    http://www.expatica.com.
    belgium.asp
Community Help Service   http://www.expats.com/chs

CULTURAL WEB SITES

The website http://ourworld.compuserve.com/homepages/Tielemans/ hp4marc. htm has a listing of famous Belgians, though if you read French you'll find that http://califice.net/belge/_is much more comprehensive and also has links to great listings and websites on Belgian beer, chocolates, cartoons, etc.

The website http://houbi.simplenet.com/belpop/ is a very comprehensive Belgian rock and pop archive.

WEIGHTS, MEASURES AND STANDARDS

This book uses the metric system as you'll find it in Belgium:
1 kilometer = 0.62 miles
1 meter = approximately 3.28 feet
1 inch = approximately 2.54 centimeters
1 kilogram = 2.21 pounds
1 ounce = 28.35 grams
In Flanders, a *pond* = 500 grams
1 litre = 2.11 U.S. pints = 1.76 British pints
1 U.S. gallon = 3.79 litre
1 Imperial Gallon = 4.55 liters
Electricity is 220V, 50Hz, plugs have two (unearthed) or three (earthed) round pins
Videos work on the PAL system
Time zone is GMT+1 (+2 from the last Sunday of April to the last Sunday of October)

VISAS AND PERMITS

Information on visas is available from the **Alien's Office** (tel 02 206 1300 http://www.just.fgov.be) and the **Foreign Affairs Ministry** (tel 02 501 8111 http://www.diplobel.fgov.be/Visitors/Visa/Menu_EN. htm). Regulations regarding the application for and use of visas, work permits, and professional cards are described in detail at http:// www.diplobel.org/australia/Sydney/English/visitors/visa.htm and http://diplobel.fgov.be/China/English/html/visa.html. Although these are primarily aimed for applicants in Australia/China respectively, they both help to clarify the sort of specifics that any individual consulate may require of you.

Contact the **Ministry of Middle Classes** (tel 02 208 3211 http: //www.cmlag.fgov.be) or access the website http://citizens.eu.int/ cgi-bin/fsprint.cgi for more information on identity cards and residence permits.

MEDICINE
INAMI   http://inami.fgov.be/

SCHOOLS

Useful information on schools appears in an annual schools' guide that comes free for subscribers of *The Bulletin* every April and in their twice yearly *Newcomers'* guide. You can also visit http:// www.xpats. com or http://www.kuleuven.ac.be/soi/schoolbe.htm for more information.

For a full listing of Francophone primary schools in each commune, visit http://www.agers.cfwb.be/org/fondam/commune.asp. The website http://www.restode.cfwb.be/org/index.htm provides information on schools in the French community including details of special facility schools (in French). For details on the compulsory education sector, visit the website http://www.agers.cfwb.be/ORG/ ensoblig/sommaire.htm (also in French).

Etudes, Toutes Directions produced annually by Le Vif L'Express is a useful Francophone booklet that helps with further education and career choices. Call 02 640 8008 for a copy.

Information on Flemish schools is available on http://www.ond.vlaanderen.be/, or the smaller and less comprehensive English language site, http://www. flanders.be/public/flanders/education/index.asp.

INFORMATION ON EVENTS

Tourist Offices

Contact tourist authorities for the most updated schedule of events. The central **Belgian Tourist Office** is helpful (tel 02 504 0390 then press "4" for information in English) and can answer many questions on the more major events.

For less widely publicized events (of which there are thousands), call the local or provincial tourist offices or refer to the Wednesday edition of *Le Soir* newspaper whose "MAD" section has a "what's on" listing that covers events nation wide (in French).

TOURISM WEBSITES

General	http://www.belgium-tourism.net/
Events in Belgium	http://www.belgianexperts.com/be_calendar.htm
Flanders tourist office	http://www.toervl.be/en/intra_0_en.shtml
Flanders/Brussels	http://www.visitflanders.com
Wallonia/Ardennes/	http://www.belgique-tourisme.net Brussels
	http://www.idearts.com/events/ is also good for events in Wallonia—click on the month required

Provincial Tourist Offices

Antwerp	tel 03 240 6373
	http://www.tourprovantwerp.be
Brabant Wallon	tel 02 351 1200 fax 1300
	http://www.brabantwallon.be
Hainaut	tel 065 36 0 464/069 354 285
	http://www.ideta.be (Tournai area)
Liège	tel 04 232 6510
	http://www.ftpl.be
Limburg	tel 011 237 450
	http://www.toerismelimburg.be
Luxembourg	tel 084 411 011
	http://www.ftlb.be
Namur	tel 081 749 900
	http://www.ftpn.be
Oost Vlaanderen	tel 09 267 7020
Vlaams Brabant	tel 016 267 620
West Vlaanderen	tel 050 380 296
	http://www.westtoerisme.be

Town Tourist Offices

Most towns also have their own tourist office. Numbers are listed below. Websites are usually in the form http://www.townname.be Site standards vary considerably: Poperinge, Spa and Tournai's sites are relatively good and have English language options.

Aalst, 053 732 270; **Aarschot**, 016 569 705; **Antwerp**, 03 232 0103; **Arlon**, 063 220 256/216 360; **Bastogne**, 061 215 790 /212 711; **Binche**, 064 336 727; **Bouillon**, 061 466 257; **Bruges**, 050 448 624; **Brussels**, 02 513 8940; **Charleroi**, 071 866 152; **Chaudfontaine**, 04 361 5630; **Dendermonde**, 052 213 956; **Diksmuide**, 051 519 146; **Dinant**, 082 222 870; **Durbuy**, 086 212 428; **Eupen**, 087 553 450; **Geel**, 014 570 950; **Genk**, 089 309 561; **Gent**, 09 225 3641; **Hasselt**,

011 239 540; **Opheylissem/Hélécine**, 019 655 100; **Herenthals**, 014 219 088; **Huy**, 085 212 915; **Ieper** (Ypres), 057 228 584; **Jodoigne**, 010 819 951; **Kortrijk**, 056 239 371; **Leuven**, 016 211 539; **Liège**, 04 221 9221; **Lier**, 03 488 3888; **Maaseik**, 089 566 372; **Malmédy**, 080 330 250; **Mesen**, 057 445 040: **Mons**, 065 335 580; **Oostduin-kerke**, 058 532 121; **Ostend**, 059 701 199; **Oudenaarde**, 055 317 251; **Passendale**, 051 770 441; **Poperinge**, 057 334 081; **Roeselare**, 051 262 450; **St-Niklaas**, 03 777 2704; **St-Truiden**, 011 701 818; **St-Vith**, 080 221 137; **Seraing**, 04 336 6616; **Soignies**, 067 347 376; **Spa**, 087 795 353; **Stavelot**, 080 862 706; **Tongeren**, 012 390 255; **Tournai**, 069 222 045; **Turnhout**, 014 443 355; **Verne**, 058 330 531; **Verviers**, 087 307 926; **Visé**, 04 379 6263; **Waterloo**, 02 354 9910; **Westerlo**, 014 545 428

BOOKSHOPS

The biggest bookshop in Brussels is the cavernous French-owned **FNAC** on a special floor of the City2 shopping centre, off the rue Neuve. For books specifically in English the main Brussels choices are **Waterstones** at Adolphe Max 71-75 (http://www.waterstones.co.uk), **Sterling Books** at 38 Wolvengracht (http://www.sterling-books.be) and **The Reading Room** at 503 Ave George Henri. For travel books, try the **Anticyclone des Açores** (http://www.anticyclonedesacores.com) which has a superb range in a variety of languages, or the **7ème Continent** in Waterloo (Chaussée de Bruxelles 407B, Waterloo, tel 02 353 0230).

For second-hand books and books at reduced prices (mainly Flemish but with a selection in English) try **De Slegte** on the rue des Grands Carmes in Brussels or look into **Evasions** across the street at the corner with the rue du Midi (plenty of old guides to Brussels and Belgium, mostly in French). Rather like Hay-on-Wye in England, **Redu** in the Ardennes has become known as a "book village" and has summer and Easter book fairs with shops staying open into the night (call 061 656 516). The Belgian version of Amazon on-line bookshop is http://www.proxis.be which stocks books in English as well as French and Dutch. Their prices are typically somewhat higher than Amazon or Barnes & Noble, but this is offset by their recent decision to drop delivery charges from 60BEF per book to none at all.

TRANSPORT

Driving in Belgium

Feu Vert...' is a the name of a French language CD ROM and book giving practice exercises to prepare you for the tests. Sample questions are available on-line at http://www.brocom.be/FR/brocom framesettest.htm. For driving test centres, inquire at GOCA rue de la Technologie 21-25 1080 Bruxelles, tel 02 469 0600.

The website http://brussels.interconti.com/location/driving3.html provides details on drink driving limits in Belgian. If you want to get temporary or transit plates for your car, the website http://www.vici.fgov. be/en/diven/diven.htm gives clear step by step instructions in English.

Bus Companies

STIB/MIVB	tel 02 515 2000
(Brussels buses, trams	http:// www.stib.be (French)
and metro)	http://www.mivb.be (Flemish)
De Lijn	tel 015 440 711 / 03 218 1406
(Flemish bus company)	
TEC	tel 010 480 404 / 08 125 3555.
(Wallonia buses)	http://www.tecbw.com for Brabant Wallon services
Eurolines (international)	information tel 02 538 2049 bookings tel 02 203 0707 http://www.budgettravel.com.eurbus. htm

	http://www.gobycoach.com (from U.K.)
Midi Tours	tel 02 511 9394
(buses to Spain, North Africa)	
Tourbus (bus to Prague)	http://www.tourbus.cz/mezinar/000009.html

Trains

Belgian railways	http://www.b-rail.be
Thalys	http://www.thalys.com
(high speed trains to Paris/Amsterdam)	
Eurostar	http://www.eurostar.com
(high speed trains Brussels–Lille–London)	
Eurotunnel	http://www.eurotunnel.co.be
(operator)	
TGV/French railways	http://www.sncf.com/indexe.htm
Vennbahn steam railway	tel 087 858 285
	http://www.vennbahn.de
Italian railways	http://www.trenitalia.com
German railways	http://www.bahn.de
Dutch railways	http://nsr.ns.nl/reisplan2a.asp

Ferry Links to U.K.

Dover ferries site	http://www.topsy.demon.co.uk/dover/ferries.html
Hoverspeed	http://www.hoverspeed.co.uk (hovercraft/Seacat)
Norfolk Line	http://www.norfolkline.com
(boats, Dunkerque–Dover)	
P&O North Sea	http://www.ponsf.com
(boats, Zeebrugge–Hull)	
P&O/Stena Line	http://www.posl.com
(ferries Calais–Dover)	

Seafrance	http://www.seafrance.net
(ferries Calais–Dover)	tel 02 549 0882

Airlines and Airports

Antwerp Airport	http://www.antwerpairport.be
Brussels Airport	http://www.biac.be

flight info is available by teletext on RTBF1 TV page 597/598

Charleroi Airport	http://www.charleroi-airport.com/eng/
Liège Airport	http://www.liegeairport.com
	(charters/cargo)
Sabena	tel 02 723 2323
	http://www.sabena.be
Ryanair	http://www.ryanair.com
Virgin Express	tel 02 752 0505
	http://www.virgin-express.com
VLM	http://www.vlm-airlines.com/uk/
Citybird	http://www.citybird.com

Travel Agents

USIT Connections	http://www.connections.be
	English language tele-sales 02 550 0100
Airstop/Taxistop	http://www.taxistop.be/airstop/ea_frame.htm
	tele-sales 070 233 188

FOOD AND DRINK

The website http://www.resto.be is a great site that allows diners to comment upon their culinary experience, and to read the comments of others. While there is a certain suspicion of some restaurateurs adding their own eulogies at times, the site remains a generally good source of unbiased feedback. For some imaginative variants of

Belgian speciality recipes by top chefs, visit http://saveurs. sympatico. ca/ency_9/belgique/menu.htm.

Beer and Booze

Using the internet you can choose from an extremely well-catalogued choice of 400 beers on http://www.beermania.be, although you'll need to buy about 40 bottles to offset the minimum shipping fee of some 700BEF. The website http://www.belgianshop.com/en/ offers a similar if expensive service priced in dollars and aimed at export. There's a good internet beer site at http://www.dma.be/p/bier/beer.htm.

The "beer escort" site http://www.belgianstyle.com/mmguide/ offers practical help on how to track down the rarest beers, as well as giving notes on tastings, glasses etc. and links to all major brewery websites.

You can visit the **National Gin Museum** at 19 Witte Nonnenstraat, Hasselt, (closed Mondays). The **Feller Maitrank** factory can be visited by appointment (tel 063 224 166).

OVERNIGHT ACCOMMODATION

Gîtes de Wallonie produces listings books of some 550 *gîtes* and 300 *chambres d'hôtes*. Gîtes de Wallonie is located at Avenue Prince de Liège 1, B-5100 Namur, tel 081 311 800 fax 31 02 00. Their website (http://www.gitesdewallonie.net) has an English language function and lists their properties but you have to know pretty much where you want to go as listing is by area and town. For a smaller selection, free photo brochures with 320 *gîtes* and 125 *chambres d'hôtes* in rural Wallonia, are available through **Agritourisme**, rue de la Science 23-25, B1040 Bruxelles, tel 02 230 7295 fax 4251 agricole.belge @skynet.be.

You can also obtain the relevant information at **UTRA-UTA Tourisme Rural**, Chaussée de Namur 47, B-5030 Gembloux, tel 081 600 060 fax 0446 upa@win.be. A roughly equivalent brochure for

Flanders is available from the **Flemish Rural Tourism Federation** at Minderbroederstraat 8, B3000, Leuven.

MONEY MATTERS

Tax Reforms and Licenses

General taxes	http://premier.fgov.be/policy/e_beleid sverkln01.html#f)
Inheritance taxes	http://minfin.fgov.be/uk_memento/203.html
Car radio and TV licenses	http://www.redevances.cfwb.be

Banks

If you want a simple bank for keeping your Belgian currency and an account to activate your Mister Cash card, **Argenta** (http://www.argenta.be) is worth considering. They offer an unusually friendly personal service and better than average interest on accounts. However, they have limited branch network and do not offer many standard services that you'd get from any of the bigger banks (e.g. cashing traveller's checks). If you need these service, you might try **KBC** (http://www.kbc.be/ expats), **BBL** (http://www.bbl.be), and **Citibank**, which also provides a banking guide for expatriates, free of charge (fax 02 626 5624).

TELEPHONE COMPANIES

Belgacom	tel 0800 558 00 (in English)
	http://www.belgacom.be
Telnet	tel 0800 660 00
	http://www.telnet.be
	Offers a wide range of local and long distance calls in Flanders

Mobile Phones

Proximus   tel 02 205 4000
       http://www.proximus.be
Mobistar   tel 0800 959 53
       http://www.mobistar.be
Orange   tel 0800 204 86
       http://www.orange.be

INTERNET PROVIDERS

Wanadoo http://www.wanadoo.be
Skynet   http://www.skynet.be
For a complete list of providers consult http://www.ispa.be
The website http://www.twigger.be allows you to gain access to your inbox on any Belgian server (e.g. if you're at a cybercafé).

COURIER MAIL SERVICES

DHL   tel 02 715 5050
FedEx   tel 0800 135 55
TNT   tel 070 233 633
UPS   tel 0800 128 28

FURTHER READING

The selection here makes no claims to be comprehensive, but reflects what I have personally found to be most helpful and enlightening. Although sources in local languages tend to be even more useful, I have largely restricted the list to publications in English.

CULTURE—GETTING A FEEL

The best way to get a feel for a culture is to laugh sympathetically at its foibles rather than dissect it academically. If you don't have the time to do so in person, there are two particularly fine, lighthearted introductions to the Belgian people that do so for you:

Xenophobe's Guide to the Belgians by Anthony Mason (1996, Ravette Books)
Lots of genuine insights on the people and culture. When I first read this little book, I wondered whether the author knew my wife and her family. I hadn't realized until then how typically Belgian they were!

A Tall Man in a Low Land by Harry Pearson (1998, Little, Brown and Co).
Pearson, a columnist and cycling fan, decides to take a long holiday in Belgium. What? A long holiday? In BELGIUM? "The concept was just too alien and difficult," he explains. "It was as if we had tried to explain the theory of special relativity to a three year old." The resultant book is a brilliant series of well-informed swipes and chortles at everything from Walloon pet shops to racing pigeons to Flemish garden gnomes. Highly recommended, although non-British readers may struggle with some of his funniest analogies.

In the Belgian Chateau: The Spirit and Culture of a European Society in an Age of Change by Renée C. Fox (1994, Ivan R. Dee Inc.)
This book is an interesting attempt to look at the traditional class system within the Belgian context, but considered a little dated by some Belgian readers.

SETTLING IN

At the risk of repeating the fact a little too often, expatriates in Belgium will thank themselves for taking a subscription to the weekly magazine ***The Bulletin***. Call 02 373 9909 or fax 02 375 9822, for subscription details. The subscription fee currently stands at 4000BEF/year, delivered within Belgium, 5950BEF for the rest of Europe, and 8950BEF for the rest of the world. Subscribers receive the very useful magazine ***Newcomer*** twice yearly. It's packed with practical information about the way systems work here, and lists contacts for a variety of menial but important day to day needs. Another useful source is ***Expats in Brussels***, an annual guide.

TRAVEL AND ACCOMMODATION GUIDES

In English, the ***Blue Guide*** is the best travel guide for its sheer weight of facts, places, and historical detail, although it does not necessarily give practical advice for accommodation options and restaurants. The *Blue Guide* also has some very good town plans and has a fairly comprehensive color atlas which is much more useful than a small country map. The ***Michelin Green Guide*** is likewise good but less detailed. The ***Rough Guide*** seems slightly weak overall, missing out on many of the smaller towns, but is pretty good for town maps and OK on practical detail. A ***Lonely Planet Guide to Belgium and Luxembourg*** has just been published. It seems to be unusually thorough. There are also several guides concentrating on Bruges,

Brussels, and Antwerp—a particularly interesting choice is Derek Blyth's *Flemish Cities Explored*.

Free tourist pamphlets give very comprehensive hotel and camping site listings and many are available in English. If you read French or Flemish your choice is vastly wider; guide books and thematic picture books are written on pretty much any region, city, or aspect of Belgium. For great B&B and hotel recommendations, try *Maisons d'Hôtes de Caractère/Karaktervolle Gastenkamers* or the very practical *Logis de Belgique*, a little sister volume to the great *Logis de France*. The *Ippa Guides* are excellent for their coverage on thematic interests (festivals, castles, abbeys, etc.) and have plenty of glorious photographs without skimping on detailed background information. However, the guides lack maps and have small indexes.

FOOD

For selecting restaurants, the excellent annual *Delta Guides* are incredibly thorough. Recipe books include the *Everybody Eats Well in Belgium Cookbook* by Ruth Van Waerebeek-Gonzalez (1996, Workman Publishing Company). It has over 200 Belgian recipes from fancy fruit-meat counterpoints to good old meatballs in beer. The book offers ingredient alternatives for dishes where items (e.g. sorrel) may be hard to find. The *Belgo Cookbook* is also worth a try.

HISTORICAL

Histoire de Belgique is still the classic historical guide to Belgium, though written in the 1950s. Four volumes, in French.

History of the Low Countries by J. C. H. Blom & E. Lamberts (Editors), James C. Kennedy (Translator) (1999, Berghahn Books) A well-illustrated collection of pieces by specialists in various fields, translated such that it manages to maintain a very readable consistency of style.

The Dutch Revolt by Geoffrey Parker (1989, Viking Penguin)
One of those rare history books which manages to keep a sharp analytical focus yet remain as thrilling to read as any good adventure novel. Gives a very broad feel for the background and history of the whole epoch as well as the two decades specifically described. As the author quickly makes explicit, the title is a misnomer—there was not one but three main revolts between 1566 and 1581.

The Low Countries in Early Modern Times by Herbert Rowen (1972, Macmillan)
A specialist collection of translated source documents rather than a history book per se, focusing somewhat more on the Netherlands than on Belgium. But some fascinating snippets include Herman Ghijsen's 1663 analysis of the economic dangers that would result should France grab Flanders (which it did in 1667).

Medieval Flanders by David Nicholas (1992, Addison Wesley Longman)
A survey of Flemish life and times with interesting quotations from contemporary documents, of which many have not been previously translated into English. Pitched at the reading level of higher education, but readable nonetheless.

Lion Rampant by Robert Woollcombe (1994, B&W Publishing)
Flemish nationalism considered.

BIOGRAPHICAL

The King Incorporated by Neal Ascherson (1999, Granta)
An intriguing attempt to understand King Leopold II without merely judging him as the monstrous dictator of the Congo. Meanwhile it gives you all you need to know about explorer Henry Morton Stanley's sex life, and the tearful fears that plagued it.

The Coburgs of Belgium by Theo Aronson (1968, Cassell)
Written in 1968 but reprinted more recently, this book gives readers a glimpse of the lives of the Belgian kings and those of their extraordinary extended family for the period until Baudouin's accession.

Paul Delvaux: Surrealizing the Nude (Essays in Art and Culture) by David Scott (1993, Reaktion Books)
Illustrated attempt to work out the importance of Delvaux to 20th century art and why he had to keep on painting his naked wife against classical landscapes.

HISTORICAL LITERATURE
If you read a single historical novel about Belgium, the obvious choice is Hugo Claus's epic ***The Sorrow of Belgium***. It manages to handle the topics of Flemish nationalism and Nazi collaboration with great sensitivity, woven into a day-to-day tale of a teenage schoolboy during World War II. This book is a brave attempt at keeping all the characters ambivalent—no heroes, no baddies, just real people muddling through.

The Shovel and the Loom by Carl Friedman, (1996, Persea Books)
A tale set in Antwerp's old Jewish quarter about a family torn between trying to forget wartime horrors and to salvage memories. The movie *Left Luggage* starring Isabella Rossellini and Maximilian Schell was based on this book.

265

THE AUTHOR

Elliott first visited Brussels at the grand age of nine and blames the Atomium for a misguided childhood fascination with chemistry. Enlightened Belgian cousins revealed to him the charms of Kwak, soukous music and the Forêt de Soignes, yet he fled east. But after three years of squid and blues harmonica, Elliott left his temporarily adopted Japanese island exile, heading home for the U.K. So far he's only made it as far as Belgium where he's been living ever since with a very special woman who found him at a Turkmenistan camel market. Elliott has written several guidebooks, including *Asia Overland* (1998) and *Azerbaijan with Georgia* (1999, 2001).

INDEX

7334